William + Karyn Logan.

Norah Bradford

WHEN TIME IS TAKEN

Dedication

I dedicate this book to my loved Robert.
To Ken Campbell who also sadly lost his life that fateful day.
To my precious daughter, son-in-law and my grandchildren.

Published by
Maurice Wylie Media
Your Inspirational Publisher

Publisher's statement: Throughout this book the love for our God is such that whenever we refer to Him, we honour with capitals. On the other hand, when referring to the devil, we refuse to acknowledge him with any honour to the point of violating grammatical rule and withholding capitalisation.

For more information visit
www.MauriceWylieMedia.com

Disclaimer: Some names have been changed to protect individuals.

Acknowledgements

I want to thank my Church family for your love and prayers.
Thank you to the Minions prayer team for your love and faithfulness.
Thank you to all the people who have loved, supported,
and prayed for me over many years.

Thank you all.

Endorsements

I first met Robert and Norah through the Vanguard Political party and that was the beginning of a wonderful relationship between us; that led to my often visiting his home in the ensuing years.

Their energy and drive to see justice and fairness across the classes came from Robert's upbringing in a working-class home, and gave them an understanding of life at the grass roots.

They also were beacon carriers against unfairness in the different communities whether Catholic or Protestant. They never asked, 'what religion are you? 'They only asked, 'How can we help? 'People saw that Robert helped everyone equally.
Robert drew support from both communities and was elected to the House of Commons at Westminster twice.

But the enemies of Northern Ireland hated him for standing up for both communities and on 14th November 1981 murdered a great colleague and friend of mine.

Like too many other people in Northern Ireland, his life was cut short by terrorists.

He made a significant contribution to politics in Northern Ireland. Had his career not been so cruelly ended I have no doubt his contribution would have been much greater.

This book written by Norah will express to many that they don't stand alone; that their partners are not forgotten and together they will stand strong in this time where it seems others want their names to be forgotten.

I salute you Norah that through that darkness and pain that you have kept going raising your daughter who was left fatherless and honouring Robert through your life.

Lord David Trimble
First Minister Northern Ireland 1998-2002.
Nobel Peace Prize Winner 1998.

In this impactful account of life, love and loss set during the turbulent years of the Northern Irish Troubles Norah vividly paints a portrait of a reality little understood by those outside the time or geography of those dark days of violence. Many who lived through those terrible years of pain, suffering and trauma *(Rose included)* will recognise instantly the recollections, moods and emotions captured on these pages. Norah's story move's one to tears. But it does much more than that. It offers the reader a challenge and a hope. The challenge? That we must face the darkness bravely even when the questions linger. The hope? *Post Tenebris Lucem* 'After Darkness there is Light'. The arc of Norah's pen sweeps beyond the shores of Northern Ireland to touch the lives of the many who identify in different but similar ways with her experiences. Scripture records *'But as for you, you meant evil against me; but God meant it for good, in order to bring it about as it is this day, to save many people alive' Genesis 50:20 NKJV.*

Thank you Norah for embodying that truth!

Pastors Rose and Kevin Sambrook
Rhema Restoration Ministries, Northern Ireland.

Robert Bradford was to become a very close personal friend when we trained together for the Methodist ministry. He was incredibly gifted and generous to a fault, and never forgot his humble roots. Although we ultimately went in different directions our friendship continued.

I still recall where I was on that dark November day in 1981 when he was murdered by terrorists. Norah's story is deeply moving. She has made an incredible journey of faith discovering how forgiveness has released her from hurt and anger; placing Robert's death into the hands of God who will make the ultimate judgment. This book also provides a social history of the time and is a reminder to a younger generation that if we don't learn from history we are bound to repeat it.

Rev. Jim Rea
Methodist minister, retired, Belfast, Northern Ireland.

I first met Norah Bradford at a Christian counselling course in 2000 and was inspired by her care for others. Norah has 3 great passions: - Jesus, serving Him, and seeing people fulfil their God given potential. She has first-hand life experiences of traumatic events and longs to see others, who have had similar experiences, set free from the hurt, anger and guilt it causes. Walking in this freedom has produced great wisdom, enthusiasm for life and such tremendous creativity both in her painting and writing, it can only inspire. She writes with honesty and truth being vulnerable in her quest to help anyone who finds themselves in hard places. This book is no surprise to me as she knows that if He brought her freedom, by being faithful to His call to write this, He can do it for anyone who reads it and that is her greatest desire.

Rosie McCorkell
Missionary for AIM and OMS.

Norah has an engaging style of drawing people along on the journey with her as she candidly speaks of not only a public and private life story but the intimate story of her heart. This poignant narrative is the human story behind the politics. It presents not only an historical account, a window into the world of a public profile man and his family but also unites the hearts of those who like Norah have been afflicted by the human tragedy of terrorism. The final presents a message of hope for freedom that is not found in revenge but forgiveness. I honour the courage Norah has demonstrated in writing this book.

Pastor Beverley Dales
Adv Dip CFT, Grad Cert CFT, Life Care Services, Principal Master Trainer of Mental Health First Aid, Australia.

Rev. Robert Bradford had a powerful influence and impact on my life as a young minister. I met Robert in the mid-1970s when he visited the States on several occasions to connect with churches in the Methodist tradition. I was privileged to hear Robert speak in religious and secular settings. He spoke with a calling, boldness and authority that only God could give whether in churches or in secular settings. Passion and conviction always showed.

His Northern Irish accent I will never forget and as for his laugh, that was contagious. I will always remember and cherish the times I was able to sit and talk with him one on one. He listened intently and shared wisdom and encouragement that I so needed at that time. I will never forget those short moments I shared with this great man who took time out to talk and listen to me.

His life was taken too soon from us. I am reminded of Revelation 14:13, *"Yes, says the Spirit, they will rest from their labor, for their deeds will follow them."*

Robert is no longer with us, but his deeds still follow in our hearts and lives.

In 1981 the world lost a dynamic man; I lost my friend.

Rev. Johnny Hankins
Methodist minister, retired. Louisiana USA.

For many people across the United Kingdom and beyond, The Troubles of Northern Ireland are slipping into the past and into the history books. But for someone like Norah Bradford the past will always be in the present and her noble desire is to see a better, fairer and more peaceful future. *"When Time is Taken"* is her powerful testimony to the memory of her late husband, Robert, and her continuing struggle to fulfil the ideals for which they both worked and in which they both believed passionately.

I had the privilege of meeting the Reverend Robert Bradford in 1972 while he was the minister of Suffolk Methodist Church on the Stewartstown Road, and I was a platoon commander patrolling in the Andersonstown and Suffolk area of West Belfast. For those who do not know the area, at the time it was the scene of great tension and periodic intense violence between the Loyalist and Republican communities. I came to greatly respect the local leadership of Robert Bradford and his desire for peaceful community relations. It was therefore no surprise to learn later that he had entered the House of Commons to pursue his work at an even greater level. It was, of course, with the heaviest heart that one heard of his murder at the hands of terrorists. Such a tragedy and apparently such a waste of a good life.

In her book, Norah has picked up the torch of hope that was torn from Robert's hands on the day of his assassination. That good life that was Robert continues through Norah. *"When Time is Taken"* is a searingly honest book, written from a loving heart but with a determination of steel. There are injustices to be challenged and a pursuit of truth to be championed. Norah Bradford does not hold back, and she is to be commended and respected for that. This book is a most compelling read and will challenge many people's preconceptions of what really happened during the dark days of The Troubles.

Richard Dannatt
General the Lord Dannatt GCB CBE MC DL Chief of General Staff (Head of Army) 2006-2009.

Contents

Foreword

For most people who listened to the daily news during Northern Ireland's blackest days, the announcement of another killing left a depressing feeling of sadness and helplessness. The most caring in our society will have offered up a prayer for the bereaved or verbally expressed their grief and sorrow to those they met. For some, when they listened to the personal horrific story of a life stolen from those they loved, abhorrence and heartache will have attended their tears.

Yet, when the victim was somebody we knew, loved, respected and was part of our lives the emotions were so much greater and the anguish so much harder to carry.

This is a personal and powerful narrative of Norah's life with Robert – the happy times when they met and the precious moments they spent together, the challenges they faced both while Robert was in the Ministry and in Parliament, and their shared walk and relationship with Christ.

In what is a heart-rending account of the loss of her cherished husband, Norah shares with us a dimension much less broadcast. It is the story of those most directly and closely impacted by such an event and the struggle to come to terms with the sheer awfulness of the murder and the courageous journey to find a purpose and reason to continue without hatred. This journey is not taken in a vacuum or void. It takes place against an ongoing terror campaign with the repeated recalls as many others become the victims of evil men.

I knew Robert well, we were Parliamentary neighbours and friends.

We were members of different parties but that was a distinction that neither of us cared about. Our two constituencies adjoined each other and we worked together on matters that effected both our constituents. Often we would have met around a graveside or at the home of a victim of terrorism. This was a vicious and evil campaign of gratuitous violence. In a small community like Northern Ireland the murder of 3,500 people and the maiming of almost 40,000 citizens has an impact in almost every home. If those statistics were taken in proportion to the population of the USA more than 650,000 people would have been killed and 7.5million people maimed. But if this book tells us anything it is that statistics do not tell the whole story.

Robert's death was one of those 'Do you remember what you were doing when …?" moments. I do. I was at home when a friend who works in the emergency services rang to inform me of the shooting. I was stunned. The days that followed demonstrated just how highly the people of Northern Ireland regarded Robert and how much they felt his loss.

When you leave this book down you will feel both joy and sadness. The joy comes from Norah's enduring faith and strength of character that helped her find a path through the painful aftermath to find peace on the other side. The sadness comes from the knowledge that too many others did not.

Rt Hon Peter Robinson
Former First Minister of Northern Ireland 2008-2016.

Introduction

I am just one of many that could tell the following story of the many thousands of people in Northern Ireland and border areas of the Republic of Ireland, mainland Britain—terrorists robbed us of a loved one.

This book is not only about the death of my husband, Rev. Robert Bradford MP, but what life was like as a wife to someone who was under constant threat of death.

Like the fearful eruption and shaking of an earthquake, another world was about to be unleashed on many innocent people in Northern Ireland as the ground shook under us in the late 1960s. We now had to be careful what streets we walked, where we drove, and who was seeking to befriend us. The comfort of sitting at peace in our own armchairs at home was gone, doors were kept locked, the car checked for booby-traps (more than once a day). Terrorists declaring over our lives, "You will not live free, you will not walk free, you will not live in peace. In other words, do what we say … or *die.*"

"Normal" was a white-knuckle ride. No two days were the same, and the majority of people here in Northern Ireland lived this way. From the fear of walking past a car parked with a concealed bomb in Belfast to a lonely farmhouse in the border areas, who would be waiting for you as we opened the door to say "good morning" to a new day—the fear was real and tangible. The terrorists had cloaked our land in it, and we were being smothered.

We lived the life of being constantly alert and on guard. It made everything we did or planned to do incredibly complex and confusing.

We could not just take off for a day away without planning, thinking, for that matter trying to outthink what was planned against us.

At times we would pack a picnic into the boot of the car and travel out along a country road. Finding a field gate open, we would stop and out came our picnic. For that moment we were like a normal family in a faraway land in a newly cut field in blissful isolation from civilization, with our dogs running, then a passing car would slow down, we'd hold our breath till it moved on, breathe, and look at each other. Had we been followed?

For the people of Northern Ireland, many of you lived as we did. The pain we have carried not just of our loved one being stolen from us but the years of lies, deceit, underhand deals, conspiracy, no proper acknowledgement of our pain. God has taken a record of those terrible injustices.

Each of you are important. You who have held the candle for your loved one whether through loss of life or limb, assassination or their future through PTSD, none of it has been forgotten. None of it is missed!

Chapter One

A Teenager in Love

With six plates of food balanced, two on my hands and another on each forearm, our table was eating faster than others. It was a ravenous youth camp. The food disappeared fast and noisily. My first experience of explosive teens and twenties was a free, fun-filled week.

It was 1964. I was 16 and loving it.

"Craic" (that's fun in Northern Irish) was the order of the day. Yes, we had teaching and quiet times, all in an atmosphere of joy!

My first Methodist Missionary Conference was that Summer School week at Mourne Grange, Kilkeel. The rest of the year it was a boy's boarding school, and it made a tremendous impression on me. At last, I was a person in my own right rather than being continually introduced as someone's daughter or sister. People were happy to accept me for myself. I made many friends and enjoyed the explosive exuberance of the young people. The week had flown by, yet we packed so much into it.

Communion service was in the little grey chapel in the grounds on Sunday morning as the week came to a close. An appeal was made for anyone who wanted to commit their life to the Lord. I knew beyond a shadow of a doubt that this meant me. I couldn't wait to get to that communion rail. I probably stood on people's toes trying to get out of the narrow wooden pew, but I didn't have time to wait for people to move. I trembled at the presence of the Lord as I knelt and committed my life into His hands. It is a decision that has given me direction and courage continually.

The 1965 August camp in Kilkeel, in the bright summer sunshine, was where I first saw him. He had a three-piece suit on, which looked dowdy and old–fashioned.

"That's Robert Bradford," someone said.

His fair, curly hair cropped short doesn't suit him, I thought.

"Should I know him?" I said out loud.

"You know, he's an Edgehill student," she replied.

It was over a year later that I met Robert face to face. The Belfast group's Summer School reunion in October was held in our school chaplain's house. We had a time of Bible study and prayer, followed by supper and a chance to chat. I was talking to my friend Barbara, sitting cross-legged on the floor, when I became aware of him watching me. I blushed and continued talking, trying to ignore those smiling, light brown eyes framed in thick, dark-rimmed spectacles. Barbara turned to him, and he joined in the conversation. I in turn watched him. There was sparkle and life in this boy that I had not noticed on that summer day the year before.

Winter was severe that year and spring slow to arrive. One cloudy, cold day, cars began arriving at the Donaghadee manse. Barbara bounced over to me and shook her head to tell me that the boy I rather liked hadn't come. I sagged with disappointment. A few minutes later,

Robert and a few of his friends spilled out of an old Hillman Minx, and he came over to say hello. I was surprised and delighted, but I could not show it.

It was too cold and wet to face the beach as we had planned, so instead we picnicked in the manse dining room and later braved a walk around the harbour and lighthouse. We broke up into twos and threes quite naturally along the footpath. I found myself walking with Robert and another girl. As we talked and joked, time passed quickly.

The fun accelerated at the harbour, where I found myself dragged to the edge and held over the precipice. We laughed a lot on that short walk, with the wind blowing our dripping ice cream all over our clothes. I was discovering what tremendous fun this guy was. I had met few people with such wit and charm. I laughed that day until the tears ran down my cheeks. Robert slipped his arm gently around my shoulders and that of my companion. A strange tingle went down my spine which was a rather pleasant feeling. I think it was that afternoon that I fell in love with him.

Time passed slowly that summer. Boarding school wasn't much fun and was, at best, boring. I was leaning on my elbows at the library windows one grey day when a certain grubby Hillman Minx roared up the College Gardens. Its speed caught my attention as it screeched to a halt at the side gate. A girl jumped out of the passenger seat and ran up the stone steps into McArthur Hall. The car turned, collected her as she ran out and was gone as quickly as it had arrived.

I wandered up the oak panelled corridor towards the hall door, trying to look unconcerned. On the hall table was a letter addressed to me.

"No doubt you will be surprised to receive this note, almost as surprised as I am to find myself writing it.

Would it be possible to meet me for coffee sometime? Perhaps boarding poses difficulties … it might be that you might not want to make an arrangement of that nature. After all that, let me say that I would like, if at all possible, to have coffee with you on some suitable day.

Kindest regards,
Robert Bradford"

Sense told me not to respond too quickly, but I was bored, and he was nice, so he had his reply by the next post.

We sat in that old Hillman Minx at the front door of McArthur Hall. The roses in the circular flower bed were just bursting into bloom.

I couldn't get permission to leave as Robert's name was not on my parental list of suitable people with whom I could leave the premises.

Sitting in the car was unheard of but not against any written law. I could feel the indignant eyes from the staffroom window on the back of my neck. We talked of many things, finding more and more in common as time passed. The most important thing was that we both loved the Lord and were committed to serving Him. Surprisingly, we both felt drawn to missionary work in South America.

Our next date was in the city centre where we were to meet at Hoggs China shop. Both of us had borrowed blue raincoats, as we later laughingly discovered. Robert was very late. I wondered if he was coming, when he ran towards me, grabbed my hand and raced away. He had just abandoned his car at the traffic lights.

What cheek! I thought.

Life was taking on a wonderful new dimension. Waiting in school for that car to arrive was fun. Robert was now on the register as "suitable" and could drive up to the door to collect me, although we preferred the side gate where fewer people knew our business. Robert was always late and the car so caked with mud that it was hardly possible to read the number plate. The soft, leather bench seats, the gear stick on the steering column that Robert had to gently encourage to stay in place, the aroma of Old Spice that I still associate with that car, all combine with a nostalgia I feel for those carefree days. All the boys I knew with cars raced everywhere to impress their girlfriends but not Robert. He was a careful driver. He had accidentally injured a child in earlier years, and although not his fault, it had affected him deeply so that he avoided speeding.

My parents wanted to meet Robert and vet him for themselves. He was 25 and I was a naive 18-year-old. I was their last little fledgling, and they had no intention of allowing me to leave the nest early. One fateful day in July, Robert drove to Donaghadee to be introduced to them. When I heard the car, I ran out to meet him. His old XLF was sparkling in the sun. Robert looked different too. I hadn't seen him this nervous or serious before. He fixed his waves into place in the mirror for the third time, straightened his suit, ran his finger inside his collar, and clearing his throat announced, "Right, throw me to the lions."

On the walk around the house to the wide, mahogany front door, mischief bubbled over his apprehension and he stole a kiss.

"Serves you right if my dad throws you out as unsuitable because you wear lipstick," I teased.

It was a very tense meeting for me as my dad and Robert *tried* quietly to score points off each other. Robert obviously didn't want to push things too hard, and I saw him bite his lip as he kept back a cheeky retort, but the mischief was obvious in his eyes. The climax came near the end of a very quiet meal with stilted conversation, when my dad offered Robert a slice of cake.

"I'm fine, thanks," said Robert.

"I didn't ask you that," retorted Dad. "I said, 'Would you like some cake?'"

Robert swallowed hard and said, "No thank you."

At that point I was ready to kill my dad who was enjoying every minute of it. His blue eyes sparkled as he smiled at me, and I gave him a look fit to frazzle him, which almost made him laugh out loud. I can still hear myself shouting at him later, "How could you be so mean?"

He turned to look at me from his favourite armchair with a look of insulted innocence and said, "Do what, dear?"

I did not miss the twitch at the corner of his eyes and I told him so, but I loved him so much that my anger didn't last long, and we both dissolved into laughter.

"Did you see his face when I offered the cake?" Dad chuckled.

"You are rotten!" I protested.

My relationship with Robert was growing closer, and we were spending more time together. This was my A Level GCE course year, but I found it hard to settle down and study. I shared a room with a girl who worked hard and always came out with top marks. She worried terribly about me leaning on my elbows in that turret room, gazing out over the treetops in the direction of Edgehill College. My mind was far from English, Geography, Biology or indeed anything academic.

Our favourite place was a little café on the Ormeau Road called "The Gaslight." Its dimly lit interior with high-backed, red leather and tweed bench seats suited our mood, even apart from the fact that a large slice of chocolate gateau and a mug of hot chocolate only cost 1s.9d.

It was difficult to escape from school for many reasons. My father was a governor of the college, and this held me with a sense of responsibility. It wouldn't do his already damaged heart any good to be told his darling daughter was being expelled for breaking the rules.

It seems the opposite sex was taboo in those days and if not for a very understanding junior mistress, we could not have met as often as we did. We were not allowed to talk to boy boarders. To be caught behind the bicycle sheds with one, however innocently, meant almost certain expulsion. To have an outside boyfriend was considered impossible but we managed it. Concessions were creeping in through a few wise senior mistresses who were aware of the changing times.

We needed to be given more freedom. The introduction of the Duke of Edinburgh Award Scheme through Frieda McConnell and Peter Marshall was the first of these. To be allowed to walk out of the gates in jeans, anoraks and knapsacks was bliss, while those who hadn't the wit to join wound their way along the pavements in navy coats, brimmed hats and court shoes, in crocodile two by two, to decidedly fewer exciting venues.

We had regular weekend camping trips, enjoying basket and cloth weaving, makeup classes, home maintenance, canoe building in Peter's loft, where the said canoe had to be strung out the window with a pully to get it to the ground, as we couldn't get it down the stairs. On one of our canoeing weekends away, as Frieda was stepping into my canoe, she slid and went over the top into the murky but shallow water. She was furious, convinced I had tipped the canoe.

Everyone laughed till we cried which didn't help her loss of dignity!

One weekend, four of us were on a campout. I had been down the long lane to the road, waving off friends who had called, and I heard footsteps behind me in the dusk light. I looked and saw a male figure so I quickened my walk and he did too. I had a long lane and two fields to cross to our tent and by the time I was near the tent I was belting along, terrified and screaming! My friends scouted around and saw no one. I recovered and began to calm down, as I was supposed to be in charge of looking out for them. Suddenly, someone tripped over a guide rope. Well, that was too much. I grabbed an axe, charged out and chased the man right to the lane. The others were terrified. They thought I was going to kill him! I was almost angry enough to do so!

We walked to the nearby farmer's house and told our story. They surmised that it might be a disabled lad living nearby, who was a "bit nosey." They promised to watch so we gratefully returned to the tent and stayed vigilant, but no further incidents happened.

The Summer School week in August at Mourne Grange, Kilkeel, was a time to be together again. Methodist teens to twenties, leaders, visiting speakers, and missionaries home on furlough occupied the main house which was divided into many dorms and bedrooms and other houses on the grounds. Some boys slept in the basement gym while others slept in the monastery, a large house situated at the end of the back lane which was also the exit to the main road.

Others were in the "cabin," a small, wooden, one-story building with camp beds, and any overspill was in the sports hall pavilion, the least favourite place as it was cold and damp with a hard, concrete floor.

The day began with prayers and breakfast. Then at 10 a.m., we had an hour-long talk from a visiting speaker. You had to provide your own cushion for the wooden benches which seemed to grow harder as the week progressed no matter how inspiring the speaker. After morning coffee, it was "quiet time," and everyone split up to be on their own. It was a time to think over what had been said, to meditate on scripture, to talk quietly to the Lord and listen to His voice. As the days passed, I could sense that Robert was drawing away from me. Was I clinging too much? I wanted to spend as much time as possible with him, but he didn't seem to see it that way.

Afternoons were free and the grounds were laid out with a croquet lawn, two tennis courts and a football pitch. Sports tournaments were held and everyone joined in. It didn't matter how good you were; it was all light-hearted until the semi-finals when things became serious.

I liked croquet but regarding tennis, I was one of those people with a permanent hole in my racket. Cranfield beach wasn't far away, and frequent visits were part of the week's highlights. In the evening, a visiting missionary would give an exciting talk on far off lands, strange people, strange languages and the different customs that they worked among. The light summer evenings ended with most of us walking the couple of miles into Kilkeel, steaming bags of hot chips eaten in the Café or more often at the harbour watching the fishermen clean boats and nets or head off to the Atlantic Ocean.

Saturday night was "Frivol" night. Each dorm had to produce a sketch and act it out. Some were professional and others not so good. Late that night, after all the festivities, I couldn't sleep. This week had not been as expected and my mind was uneasy. Discipline was fairly lax, and Barbara and I managed to get out via the fire escape to go for an evening stroll and chat. Somewhere on our walk we came across a group of boys on their way to raid the "cabin." Naturally, we joined in—on one condition. They were not to disturb Robert as he had to leave early the next morning for a service. We were aware we might be picked out easily in the dark in my white summer dress and Barbara's white cardigan. We climbed in through open windows at the cabin and sat on the arms of an old armchair, watching mesmerized as silent shadows flitted through the small building, overturning camp bed after camp bed. The only noise came from the inmates as they hit the hard floor with a thud. At this point I discovered that the guy I had fallen for was snoring loudly. Gradually, the spread-eagled forms began to gather their senses, and the invaders beat a hasty exit as silently as they had come. Before we managed our own escape, a light was thrown on by a bemused Robert. What a mess met his eyes. We laughed and laughed as we dashed out leaving the boys scratching their heads in bewilderment.

Final farewells were difficult. We had made some very good friends in that short week. Emotions ran high all around, and many tears were shed. We had a lift as far as Dundalk as we'd planned a week in Dublin, and that set us well on our way to Dublin taking a bus the rest of the way. I stayed with my lovely Aunt Lorna and Uncle Bob Nelson, and Robert was bunking down in the room of a friend at Trinity College. Each day together proved better than the day before. When it was just the two of us, everything seemed fine. Perhaps I had exaggerated the sinking feeling that I'd had the previous week. The weather was glorious and much warmer than the exposed Kilkeel. We visited cathedrals and many other sights.

We planned a picnic at the seaside the next day. I was preparing it when Robert arrived in a borrowed car. We had a great time together and enjoyed the picnic. We were walking up the steep road at Howth Head when we came upon a small restaurant. The notice in the window advertised, *"Gold Medal for Wheaten Bread and First Prize for Wheaten Scones."* We went in and ordered a pot of tea and some scones. It was then that we spied the actual certificates on the wall. *"1935 Gold Medal for Wheaten Bread"* and *"1937 First Prize for Wheaten Scones."*

"Do you think we will get the prize-winning entries?" We laughed.

Chapter 2

4711 Cologne and the Nurse

Robert gave me a nickname which was our wee secret. It was supposed to be endearing but it was nothing of the sort. I objected strongly but fought a losing battle. I had never been keen on my own name and almost had a complex about it as, book after book, plays and films all cast baddies as "Norah." Norah was never the beautiful heroine who got the guy; she was always the sneaky murderess who ended up in jail. So, changing my name wasn't as traumatic as it might have been. Next, he started on my nose.

"I suppose the Lord had a purpose in giving you a bent nose. After all he made Gladys Aylward small to fit in with the Chinese. I haven't heard of them but I suppose there might be a South American tribe with bent noses just like yours for us to go and minister to!"

If he had survived until then, it was because he had ducked halfway through. He was much too strong for me to consider the destruction of his wavy hair. I would bide my time and get back at him at an opportune moment.

The Duke of Edinburgh's Gold level involved a week's camp, and my friends and I were allocated Rathlin Island, a short distance off the North Antrim coast. But just to complicate the task, we were given the job of navigating the Antrim hills by compass with set destinations along the way. There were several groups of girls. Given different routes, we split up and began our hike with heavy rucksacks, camping gear, food and cooking utensils, etc. Between arguments and widely differing opinions as to the direction we next should take, we did arrive where we were meant to be and were picked up and transported to the quayside. We boarded the small ferry and found ourselves on the inhabited island, mostly bordered by high cliffs apart from the small harbour where we docked. The history was fascinating, dating back as far as 6000 B.C., with various rulers in the ensuing years.

The residents made us most welcome, and we trudged to our distant camping ground. An army squad was there assigned to help us.

Keeping them out of our tents in the middle of the night proved a more difficult battle.

Peter and Frieda were an item by then which we ribbed them about, but they did make a great leadership team. Peter tried to separate dogs in a fight and had his arm badly bitten for his trouble.

We had reasonable weather and hiked the length and breadth, charting the many shipwrecks and investigating Brian Boru's cave (the person my brother Brian was purported to be named after). Visiting the lighthouses and writing up our necessary journals to gain our award were all part of the excitement. Photos would be added later when films were developed. On the last night, a Ceilidh was organised in the local hall. The jive, quickstep and waltz I knew and loved, but when I was hauled up for a foxtrot, I grimaced. "A what-trot?!" It was a disaster, but great fun was had by all. We succeeded, and my family and a friend, who was also being presented an award, went to Buckingham Palace. We received our awards by Prince Philip himself on a sunny, summer afternoon.

Preparing for A levels was to prove challenging for me. I enjoyed Domestic Science and found the work no problem. Biology was not in the same league. Cutting up mice that I had to catch and gas was rough enough, but when I found one had been pregnant and I had murdered five or six babies, I lost all interest. I threw my project on house flies not even bothering to work out proper percentages on the figures. Needless to say, I failed Biology but as my entrance to nursing was already arranged for September, it was not dependent on my exam results. I loved Domestic Science and at that level it was much more use to me than Biology in my first-year nursing. I was also fond of my English language teacher, "Bilko" Mr. Gray, and I worked hard at his subject. His likeness to the TV character was unmistakable, and his concern for his pupils and love of teaching endeared him to us all. I had no idea that God's plan was to make me a writer!

Robert's thoughtfulness became apparent when on the first day of my "A" level exams, he dropped a lovely note in by hand.

> *"When I'm sitting exams, I somehow feel that two people are involved. This afternoon, love, three people will be involved—God, you and me—with a team like that how can things go wrong?!!!"*

The winter term of 1967 at Edgehill College was important for Robert. I had begun my nursing training and was studying too, so we both took studying slightly more seriously than before. This meant that Robert spent more time revising than the usual two days before exams, but I had to study more extensively. With little effort, Robert came out on top in most of his exams, and humility not being his strong point, I ended up reminding him frequently of his enlarging head.

On one occasion, I discovered that my dad was marking some of his exam papers, so I picked my time carefully. One of the afternoons when I was at home, I feigned innocence, brought a cup of tea for Dad into his book-lined study with its lovely sea view.

The room was darkened by the overhead veranda outside, so for extra light, a gold-flecked, angle-poised lamp lit the surface of the large, oak rolltop desk, where the familiar silver-haired figure sat. His old Harris Tweed jacket with leather-patched elbows was worn into comfortable creases. On hearing me come in, he swung round in his swivel chair, fountain pen poised in his immaculately manicured hand. He smiled over his glasses on the end of his large aquiline nose and covered the papers on the desk with his free hand. Taking the cup of tea from me he said, "They are all numbered, love. I couldn't tell you even if I wanted to!"

I responded, "I'll pick out his handwriting for you."

"No, you won't!" he said.

As I left the room, he glanced over his shoulder and said, "He's done well … as usual."

I ran back and hugged him, planting a kiss on his forehead, loving that scent of 4711 cologne.

Robert and I grew closer and closer, even writing to each other, although we lived only a couple of miles apart. In one message he wrote:

> *"There will be times when I shall surprise you, infuriate you, amuse*
> *you and enjoy doing all three, yet at the end of the day I want you*
> *to remember that I care deeply for you."*

My aunt and uncle had invited my family to join them in Cork, in the Republic of Ireland, for a week in July and we were all looking forward to the trip. I was aware of something they didn't know. Sometime before, Robert had offered to help on the Cork circuit for part of May and June.

XLF, Robert's loved and lamented Hillman Minx car, had been replaced by a suave, blue and white Ford Anglia with pointed wings, which looked much better than it behaved. A rugby international in Dublin had seemed a lovely way to spend a Saturday in April. The atmosphere was spectacular, and the game had a lot of action. Being with a crowd of friends was a real treat.

The journey home was dreadful. The car chugged its way along, suddenly showing a burst of speed and eventually settling at a velocity of 17 mph. Every half hour Robert had to stop, take off the large, round filter and try to clean it. Our speed would increase for a few miles and gradually slow down again to crawling. On the fifth or sixth stop, his frustration which had been simmering for some time boiled over. He kicked the radiator viciously, then calmly closed the bonnet and got into the car.

"Feel better now?" I asked, trying to conceal my smile.

Fortunately, he saw the funny side of it, and we collapsed into floods of laughter. It seemed we could not remedy the situation, so we decided not to let it spoil our day, and I got a lovely letter of apology in the post a few days later.

Robert was off to Cork again and we were back to letters as our only form of communication. We soon found that we could exchange two letters in four days. His fine handwriting squeezed vast quantities onto one page, so four pages of his letters were equivalent to ten of anyone else's. Having started out early to drive the long journey to Cork, he wrote that he had made Cork by 6:45 p.m.

Getting to know the West Cork folk was a delight for him. The beauty of the little country churches was not lost on him. He loved nothing better than to play the organ, conduct worship, preach and lead the singing with his melodious tenor voice, keeping the praise going at a lively pace. The smaller the church, the more he felt at home. The Cork folk warmed to this young man with his energy, charm and wit. Being entertained by Youghal's equivalent of mayor was a big landmark in his life.

"By the way, I was almost arrested by the Garda on Saturday," he wrote.

What could he have done now? I wondered.

"I was stopped for having a faulty headlight."

I was amazed that any lights were working on that particular car!

After interrogation, he said something like this to me ... "*Now oil tell yo what oil do witch ya!! Oil take yore name but yolk can forget it and it will be a name in de boke for me—Good Nought your reverence ...*" (Robert's attempt at spelling what the policeman said in a West Cork accent!)

Preaching was what he enjoyed most, and he was getting lots of practice. Working with the young people of the circuit was also just up his street. His love of football meant he carried his boots with him everywhere. He was easily accepted by the boys and girls who adored his charm. He loved to talk of many things and answer questions, especially about his Lord. His aim in life was to draw people closer to the Saviour.

He took my photo with him to Cork, and his friends thought it was rather good.

"I have told them not to expect too much because the photographer was not very good at his job!"

He was fortunate to receive any reply to that letter at all.

It was becoming clear to both of us that God had chosen us for each other. I believe nothing happens by chance and that the Lord allowed us that time apart so that we could express what we really felt about each other in writing. He'd had a couple of close girlfriend encounters before and had shied away at the last minute. He seemed to feel trapped when marriage loomed large on the horizon. He didn't fully understand what he wanted out of those "tight corners" himself. I quickly learnt not to pressure him or he would run a mile. Life with a Methodist Minister offered little materially, but that wasn't important to me, especially if our union was ordained of God. The Lord had always provided for my family in amazing ways. We never had much money in the bank, but we never wanted for any good thing. I was convinced that the Lord who had provided so far wasn't going to stop now.

Somewhere I took time to talk to the Lord and asked, "Should I marry this man, Father?"

The Lord answered, "You're picking a very rocky road."

My immediate reaction was that at least God didn't say "No!"

In my innocence, I certainly was choosing an extremely difficult path, but when you are in love you think you can cope with anything.

When Robert wrote in this vein, he was careful to add, "However I shall not say much more in this respect, for two reasons: Firstly, I can imagine you sitting or rather hopping mad; secondly, I love you too much to risk convincing you that what I say is true."

For Robert to put that in writing was a big step. Again, he would reiterate that our lives stretched ahead with so much time together.

My parents were aware by this time that he was in Cork and fully understood why I was so keen that we should all go there on holiday. Robert's suggestion that I might stay on for a further weekend was dismissed outright. I wrote very despondently.

"But, darling," he wrote, "we have lots of time, and more important still, infinite love for each other will overcome any minor disappointments in our relationship."

During my last two years at school, a petite little girl called Sally joined the boarding department. She was very young to board at only seven years and we soon discovered that her mother had died and she and her older brothers were all sent to boarding school. A real closeness grew between us.

Often when Robert arrived in his car, she would hop into his car while he waited for me. They became great friends. She was very upset when he went to Cork and wrote to tell him so. I had to include her threatening letters in with mine. He quickly wrote, asking me for her surname, thoughtfully realizing that she might like to receive her own letters. As the end of term came in sight, everyone started making plans for the holidays. Sally began to crawl back into that protective shell I had spent the last years winkling her out of. I wrote to him telling of my concern for our little friend. He told me not to worry too much, that she was probably realising how much my departure would affect her and was in a sense living it out in the present.

Soon it was Robert's birthday, and he had hoped to be given time off to come north for a lightning visit. It seemed a lifetime since he had gone away. As time grew closer for us to meet, his letters became more compelling about our close relationship, and I became excited at the thought of seeing him again. Wednesday finally arrived and I rushed out to College Gardens for the few minutes we had at supper break.

There he sat waiting. It was so good to feel his loving arms around me. I felt so safe. I was free the next day to go home so we parted that night with the thought that it was only for a few hours. Thursday was one of those days in which school dragged by. What should I wear? I changed my mind a dozen times. I finally decided on a pretty blue cotton dress and a white cardigan.

We had a beautiful meal together and then as the sun was setting, we drove towards Newtownards. The sky was ablaze with an orange-flamed sunset. Scrabo Tower was silhouetted against a glorious sky.

We drove up Scrabo hill as far as the track would allow and got out to walk. The balmy breeze was fresher at the top of the hill. Strangford Lough was a shimmering gold. *Nowhere could be more beautiful,* I thought. We walked hand in hand through the trees down the slope.

I remember thinking, in years to come I won't remember the nettles or getting green lichen on my white cardigan from the trees. We walked quietly together, and it seemed a natural progression to talk of permanent things.

"Will you marry me?" he murmured. "We will never have much money, we will probably have to live in enormous draughty manses, but I promise you, life with me will always be different. It will never be dull or ordinary. I will make it fun."

"Yes, I think I'd like that," I replied.

On the slow drive home to Donaghadee, I commented, "How do you organise such beautiful sunsets each time we meet?"

"Well, I order them specially," he said, pointing heavenward. "After all, I have a direct line."

As the time grew near for our planned family holiday in Cork, my dad's heart began to give us all cause for concern. We got together to discuss what we should do. Dad was obviously not fit for such a long journey, so it was decided that rather than disappoint Dermot and me as well as my uncle and aunt, Dermot and I should go on our own and share the driving. The day finally arrived, and we packed up Dermot's bottle green MG 1100. Mum and Dad prayed with us for journeying mercies, and we were off.

It was late when we piled into the house in Cork, dragging our loaded suitcases to our bedrooms. I was upstairs and Dermot had been allocated the small, glass conservatory off the breakfast room. The wooden shelves were filled with red and pink geraniums, green ferns and other plants at various levels of growth. How lovely to wake up in the morning to such a beautiful aroma!

I asked to use the phone and contacted Robert. He was preaching in Youghal the next morning and had arranged for me to be included in lunch afterwards. He would pick me up on his way through from Clonikilty about 10 a.m. the next morning. I came off the phone bouncing and explained the situation to my aunt, saying I hoped she didn't mind if I wasn't back until tea time. Much to my surprise she was very hesitant but finally said I could go. I dressed quickly the next day, but at breakfast I was shocked to be told that my uncle had reversed the decision. I was not allowed to go! At 19, I felt this kind of restriction was unreasonable, but my pleading fell on deaf ears.

The doorbell rang. Yes, it was him. I explained I couldn't come. His face whitened with fury, and I had to watch a dejected figure walk back out the gate. I knew he was preaching in my aunt's church in the evening and we had the rest of the week anyhow. Somehow, we would get time together.

He walked quietly up the steps to the pulpit that evening with his sermon notes carefully tucked into his Bible. A few rousing Wesley hymns set the tone for a lively time of worship, and then I settled back into the hard, wooden pew to listen to what he had prepared.

He was not known even then for his brevity, and his fully written out sermon covered ten to twelve large pages. By page four, he was in full swing as he thumped the pulpit in enthusiasm. His sheaf of white pages rose gently in the air and floated down in all directions to the carpeted floor below. My heart sank for him! The look of blind panic on his face made me want to die for him. He hesitated, then gathered his train of thought and carried on as if nothing had happened. That was the last time he took anything, apart from very brief notes, into the pulpit. His preaching improved from that day. No longer was his head buried in the papers trying to read the notes. He learned to rely on his memory. He looked up and became more involved with his audience.

Our time together for that short week was limited for two reasons: Robert had many duties on the circuit, and my relations had arranged for Dermot and me to visit some family friends and do some sightseeing which was kind of them. Our dad and mum had lived and served the Cork church. Dermot was born while they were there.

A mid-week service was being held at Huddersfield on the outskirts of Cork City in the home of the Nicholson family. I had heard about this magnificent house since I was a child and now at last I would see it for myself. As we drove up that long driveway that lovely evening, birds were trilling in the trees as we passed through acres of woodland, and rabbits scampered out of the way of the car. We had arrived, but what was this modern bungalow? Where was the large house? We were told the upkeep of the house had become too expensive and it was not practical to carry out all of the repairs that were needed. The Nicholsons had decided to build a new bungalow. It was designed with a spacious lounge so meetings could continue to be held there. As people crowded into this lovely home, they were made to feel welcome by the family. Around 30 people settled in rows of seats and the speaker was welcomed.

The reading desk he was standing at was right in front of a large picture window. A mass of tall, wild, pink foxgloves covered the slope outside, providing a magnificent backdrop. Praise and worship flowed naturally in such a beautiful setting. After supper and lots of chatting about old times, our hosts discovered our interest in "Huddersfield" and offered to show us around the old house.

As we rounded a bend in the road, the mansion came into view. Its wide stone steps led up to a glass porch. A gigantic key was turned in the heavy wooden door and we were inside an enormous hall, I felt I was walking into the film set for *Gone with the Wind*. The echoes of former grandeur were all around. Ornate ceilings, magnificent marble fireplaces and faded, embossed wall hangings all gave a feeling of a long forgotten, lost age. The floating marble staircase solely supported by the wall, with its beautiful wooden banister, made me expect at any moment to see Scarlett O'Hara sliding down it, petticoats flying. A sad house, I thought. Gone was the laughter and life from within its walls. It was a treat to visit it.

During the week, a barbeque had been arranged by the church young people. Dermot's sojourn each night in the draughty conservatory had taken its toll and he had developed a nasty septic throat. "If Dermot isn't going then I don't think you should," announced my aunt, so Dermot very kindly dragged himself out for my sake and we met Robert there. We had been given a key to get in as my aunt and uncle didn't want to wait up for us.

"You really would almost think that Norah came to Cork to see Robert and not us," my aunt indignantly confided in Dermot before we left.

She'd never had children and it was difficult for her to understand.

She had been a missionary all her life in Madras, India, and used her art to create small books of Bible stories. She retired, returned home and met a lovely widower and married very late in life. I was her bridesmaid one January in deep snow. She had made my dress of plush, dusky-pink velvet, but mistakenly cut a low "v" in the back.

Wesley Chapel Dublin was the venue, and no one closed the door, so an icy blast blew on my back through the whole ceremony. Folks must have thought I was shivering from nervousness, but no, it was from pure cold!

Now in Cork, at the youth barbeque, it was drizzling intermittently, so it took time for the fires to warm up enough to cook our sausages on sticks. As the evening progressed, Robert took me around and introduced me to some of the young people which gave me another taste of being rejected. A young, unattached minister is fair game, and a girlfriend coming on the scene was not made to feel welcome. We had no ring and it wasn't official or known, except to us, so I stuck close to him that night feeling very isolated. Meanwhile, Dermot, looking white and miserable, decided to go home early. We arranged that he would leave his window unfastened and I would get in that way. The arrangement worked perfectly, and I was not discovered. As abruptly as it began, the week ended, and we were packing up to go home.

We filled our days together with laughter, joking and having fun.

After a lot of persuasion, Robert agreed to accompany me to the nurses' "Formal" evening in December. My meagre salary of ten pounds a month didn't stretch to a formal dress, so I set about making one in turquoise-embroidered satin. The big night came and with Robert looking fantastic in his hired tuxedo, we nervously set off for the ballroom. We spent the evening tramping on each other's toes and apologising. I did, however, have a lovely dance with a childhood friend from Armagh days. He was now a medical student and very handsome. Robert was quite put out, and I thought a bit of jealousy might be good for him! The New Year was to be spent apart, much to my disappointment, as Robert and some other students had planned a mission in Castlederg.

"Do you know that your name has infiltrated as far as County Fermanagh?" he wrote. "Not only that, but the fact I was spotted at a dance with a very glamorous girl!" so some friends in nearby Fivemiletown had said.

He wrote:

"Norah, my love, the bell has just sounded to greet the New Year. My thoughts and love are yours completely, not just tonight but for forever. Write soon and keep your eyes off those medics. Don't work too hard, my love, and do take care for I cannot do without your love and inspiration."

The first draught of stations came out in the New Year with Robert set for "Cregagh." This was a very lively large city church, and we were both excited. When the next stationing confirmed this choice, we decided to pay a visit to the church incognito (i.e., without clerical collar!). Our first impressions were less than favourable but Robert was filled with enthusiasm to change the whole world, so "Cregagh" would be no problem to him.

My off-duty times didn't allow me to be present at Robert's inauguration, but he picked me up later at the hospital, bubbling over with enthusiasm. "The people are lovely, and the church has tremendous potential. If I can get the leaders' backing, I could do so much with the young people there."

Being on circuit again and able to put into practice the training of the previous four years, plus many of his own ideas, was a delight to Robert. Although the opportunity to preach didn't present itself often, Robert found plenty of outlets for his enthusiasm. Being involved in the church football team allowed him to indulge in his favourite sport, keep himself fit, and win the confidence of the young people. More and more boys were drawn into the church through football, and girls followed. Robert wanted to provide facilities for these young people and managed to persuade their leaders to give them the use of an upstairs hall for an after-church coffee bar. "The After Eight Club" was born, a whole new venture back then. He went to endless trouble to book Christian groups to sing, and he organised speakers from many walks of life. This encouraged discussion on many Christian and moral topics. He always insisted that the young people give their full attention to the short talk, as this was closest to his heart.

As time progressed, we seemed to drift apart again. During the next twelve months we had many upsets. Several times we parted and got involved in other relationships, but we always drifted back together again. My father, who had been having heart attacks over the past years, refused to be an invalid and continued with his committees and other duties when he felt at all able, and often when he didn't.

Sometimes he would travel to Belfast by bus, often standing the whole way, as the gentleman in him wouldn't sit if a lady needed a seat. He had a lovely way of "doffing" his hat to acknowledge another person. Walking through Belfast city centre, Dad would say, "Do you see that gentleman with the moustache walking towards us? He's your second cousin once removed."

He would "doff" his hat, as would the other gentleman, smile, and pass on. He had a love of ancestry and a great fund of knowledge.

He loved graveyards best and would go from grave to grave, spouting ancestry at Mum, Der and I. I'd roll my eyes and ask if we could go.

On their way to a Church Conference in Dublin in June 1969, my parents broke their journey at Portadown to stay the weekend with my brother Harold, his wife Brenda and their family. On Sunday I'd managed to be there too. As I was leaving, my dad was gently asleep in a comfy armchair with his newest grandchild sound asleep in his careful arms. On Monday, a massive coronary took my darling dad from this world and into the arms of his Saviour. I was off duty between 2 p.m. and 5 p.m. that day and had intended to go to the centre of Belfast shopping, but something held me back from leaving the building. A phone call from an assistant matron broke the shocking news to me. I stood on the landing, stunned and speechless.

I couldn't take it in.

When I'd cried and settled a bit, I realised I needed to get to Portadown.

Morley, my brother, couldn't leave his chemist shop until he found a locum to stand in, so I phoned Robert to see if he was free to give me a lift. He told me that it would be a few hours. I also phoned my friend Barbara. She and her father rushed over and stayed with me until Robert arrived. Dad's funeral was in St. Thomas Methodist Church Portadown where he had served so faithfully. It was packed as he was much loved.

This traumatic period in my life was somehow used by God to draw Robert and me together again in a way that led to a decision to become properly engaged six months later. I had nine months of training still to do, and Robert was to be ordained that month. My mother was anxious that we should not marry until I had done my final exams. We now began to think seriously about missionary work, and we made tentative enquiries with the thought of going abroad the following year. That would give us time for Robert's ordination in June, my finals in September and getting married in December.

The stationing committee in their wisdom had placed him in Suffolk Church. Neither of us had much idea of where that was, just a vague notion that it was somewhere on the outskirts of Belfast city. After a quick investigation, we located it. We were excited by the fact that we weren't to be parted. We had dreaded that he would be shipped off to some inaccessible part of the country, but here he was within easy reach of the Royal Victoria Hospital where I worked.

We discovered through the Methodist grapevine that the Suffolk people were not too happy with his appointment. They had no continuity of ministers, just short stay ministers. They argued that they needed a steady, older man who would pull them together. They certainly didn't want a younger man who would be leaving in a year's time to go to the mission field. We prayed about what we should do considering the congregation's feelings. Believing that it was right for us to be in Suffolk, we offered a promise that we would not go abroad for five years.

Robert's ordination in the Grosvenor Hall in June, in front of a packed audience, was a moving experience. Robert spoke on putting love first in the Christian life.

July arrived, but instead of heading for Suffolk, I found myself being wheeled on a trolley towards a surgical ward in preparation for removing my inflamed appendix. When I finally got back on my feet a few weeks later, I was not able to take my finals. I was, however, allowed to leave the hospital in November having served my allotted time and could take my finals externally.

Chapter 3

Robert's Journey

Torrential rain poured out of a black sky one April day in 1943, making the deaconess's journey through the muddy cobbled streets almost impossible. Soaked through, she stepped off her bike on a Belfast Street. What number had she been given? She checked her note and found the house and knocked. No answer. She tried again, and then a neighbour across the road shouted, "She's upstairs in bed, Go on in."

Pushing the front door open, she stepped into the dark hall and looked up. There on the stairs was a small, bare-legged boy scrubbing down the wooden staircase. In the bedroom were crowded five children, looking helplessly at their emaciated, haggard mother in the bed. Mrs. Bradford lay gasping, ashen faced, almost at death's door it seemed to the deaconess. On top of the mother lay the smallest child, obviously very ill also. Ushering the children out, the deaconess did her best to make the woman comfortable. The war years were not easy on anyone, but this family was suffering more than most it seemed.

As the deaconess cycled back to the mission, thoughts raced through her head. These children didn't need a holiday as she had been told, they needed much, much more.

Gradually, as Mrs Bradford realised that these people really cared, her story unfolded.

Her husband had a milk business in Donegal Pass where they lived.

As the war progressed and life in Belfast became dangerous because of the blitz, Mrs. Bradford and her six children were evacuated to Limavady. By this time, she was expecting her seventh child. On June 8, 1941, Robert Jonathan Bradford was born.

By the time she got out of hospital, she discovered that her husband had sold the milk business and vanished from Limavady. Without a penny in the world and seven children to feed, she set herself to find a home for them. A Belfast Street became that home. Things went from bad to worse. Her health, which had never been good, deteriorated.

She was hospitalized again, and her children evacuated, this time to Ballymoney. When at last she got out of the hospital, Mrs. Bradford went to fetch them.

Short sojourns in the hospital were not enough to cure the tuberculosis she had been diagnosed with. The children tried to help around the house, but the mother's strength was failing. Gradually bronchial pneumonia developed on top of the TB, which was the point at which the Deaconess arrived, and Mrs. Bradford was taken into Whiteabbey hospital. It was wisely decided then by Mrs. Bradford she should release her two-year-old Robert.

Robert was collected by Mr. and Mrs. Nicholson (also known as Sadie and Jim) and went to be fostered by them indefinitely.

40 Hunter Street, Belfast, near Sandy Row was his new home, and it was to remain so for a long time. This was a tiny two up, two down, town house, with an outside toilet and small scullery, identical to the one he had left, except that this time he had a bedroom to himself.

This took some getting used to. Times were hard for everyone, but everything the Nicholsons had was lavished on him. He had new clothes when no one else could get any and all the dinky cars he wanted. Life was looking up for this perky, curly-haired two-year-old. His cheeky smile won the hearts of many of the neighbours.

Mrs. Nicholson worked in Grosvenor Hall, Belfast Central Mission, until lunchtime each day and Robert was sent to a daycare centre until his new mum got home. He was miserably unhappy about this and left no one in any doubt about his feelings. A relation of the Nicholson's who lived at 43 Hunter Street was housebound. Uncle Bob, as Robert called him, offered to take him during the mornings.

This arrangement suited everyone, and he grew to love Uncle Bob and his sister, Aunt Liz. Aunt Lizzy Bell worked in a local laundry as an inspector and mender. Uncle Bob had been unable to leave his house since the death of his father sometime earlier. He'd developed a phobia which he managed to overcome on a few occasions when he thought Robert had been hurt or hit by another child. Aunt Liz worked long hours for very little pay, as did most working-class folk in those days.

While the Nicholsons were at work, Aunt Liz and Uncle Bob gently guided Robert along, and he spent more and more time at No 43.

Their tremendous sense of fun gave him an insatiable appetite for jokes as he grew older. There were lots of playmates in those narrow streets, with terraced houses crammed back-to-back. Rooms were unbelievably small—you couldn't even "swing a cat" as we would say.

Row upon row of red brick houses stretched in all directions off the Donegal Road and Sandy Row, in the area he now knew as home.

People ritually painted their homes and the pavement red, white and blue every year in preparation for "The Twelfth"[1] of July celebrations.

Though small, the majority of homes were immaculately clean and well furnished. Number 40 was no exception, with its neat back yard and outside privy. Young Robert displayed a great aptitude for football, and the tiny ones playing in the street caused no problem for the residents. Traffic was infrequent and sometimes took the form of the rag-man's horse and cart. His piercing cry brought the children running from their houses. For a bundle of rags, the children were given a colourful balloon.

"What colour do you want?" the rag man asked.

"Blue, please," said Robert. "I like blue."

The rickety cart bumped off again over the cobbled streets with its load of faded, worn clothes and brightly coloured floating balloons, one in sharp contrast to the other. Further down the street, the old horse stood patiently. His bones were beginning to protrude through his thick hide. Hanging his head as he rested from his weary travelling, he watched as the children scampered around him, swinging on their makeshift swing tied to a lamppost or playing "marlies" with their coloured glass marbles on the pavement.

When the time came for school, Robert attended Blythe Street Primary, which was just around the corner. For him, school was a place to gather a football team rather than a place to study. Breaktime and lunchtime were important. The rest of the day was to get through quickly and with as little effort as possible.

On Sundays, the Nicholsons took Robert to church at Grosvenor Hall, Belfast Central Mission. The large hall and gallery were always

---

1 A public holiday in Northern Ireland and also the day when Orangemen celebrate the defeat of King James by King William of Orange.

packed for those services where the rousing hymns of the Wesleys were sung with a fervour almost to lift the roof. He attended Sunday school there, and found his knowledge of the Bible expanded—when he managed to listen. In the evenings, a meal was prepared in the back hall for "down and outs," otherwise known as tramps in those days. The church people took time to speak to these folks that the world had written off. In their rags and tatters, their several coats often tied together with string, their boots with gaping holes and unsavoury odours, their tired eyes looked towards the platform where beautifully dressed young people would sing gospel songs. Someone would tell of the love of a Saviour who cared for all, and who was waiting with open arms for them. They only had to open the door of their heart to experience an unspeakable joy.

Slowly, as time grew near for the evening service, the down and outs, both male and female, would gather their possessions, their precious bundles of newspapers and rags to keep out the cold, damp nights, and go out to face another week of life sleeping on doorways or wherever they found shelter. One man, however, would turn and make his way into the large main hall for the service. He would usually sit a few rows in front of the Nicholsons. As the time for the service drew near, a beautifully dressed little girl would flounce down the aisle to sit beside the tramp. Robert guessed she was about the same age as himself. Many times he wondered about his own dad. Was that what he was like now? He had only met him once when he had come to the house just after Robert had moved in with the Nicholsons. He patted Robert on the head, gave him a sixpence and was gone again. A painful rejection welled up within him, but he fought it back down.

Robert's teacher began to take an interest in him at school and persuaded the Nicholsons to send him to elocution and music lessons.

Mr. Nicholson played a pedal organ and accordion. He made sure Robert practised for an hour every evening. His music teacher was impressed with his ability but felt a piano would give him a better grounding than the organ, so the Nicholsons managed to purchase a piano. Primitive Street Methodist Church Boys Life Brigade was just around the corner, and he started to go there with lots of the local kids. The care and discipline did them good. He quickly discovered that if he got himself thrown out, he could play football, so he was disruptive enough for him and some pals to be thrown out and then have some football fun outside. For all that, the Boys Brigade had a profound influence on his life. The Christian discipline taught there wasn't wasted on him, though the officers might have thought so at the time.

The narrow streets barely provided enough room for football and occasionally windows were broken when the boys got too enthusiastic.

One such day a fast match was in progress where goals were being scored with enthusiasm. When Robert got the ball, he dribbled it up the pot-holed street, kicked with all his might and scored.

Cheers went up from the boys, but he looked far from happy. While the ball might have gone through the goal posts, His grubby shoe had gone in the other direction and the ominous sound of tinkling glass sent the boys scattering in all directions. Robert owned up to his misdemeanour as he couldn't have explained away his missing shoe. He got off with a reprimand and paid for the window. Football was frowned upon by many residents for that very reason, so it was better to play a few streets away from home. Then, if the police chased you, you might not be so easily identified. Gaffikin Street and the streets beside the trolley bus depot were a favourite with Robert and his mates. With the dugout base for tram inspection, there were numerous places to hide if you were in danger of being chased.

Football took up every spare moment of his life and led him and his mates through the elite Malone Road to the open spaces of Barnett's

Park. There they thought they could play their cricket and football without annoying anyone, but it was not to be. Residents complained about the boys and the police arrived. They discreetly watched the boys and could see no problem but took their names and addresses anyway. Reporting back to their superiors, they were overruled, and letters were sent to their parents telling them that they were not allowed to continue their outings. Something within Robert told him, "Someday I will live up here myself. Someday I will."

The 11-plus examination loomed but there was no pressure as few of the children were expected to pass it; it was an unexpected bonus if they did. But Robert failed, despite having put in some work for it.

Just at that time an evangelistic mission was organised at the Grosvenor Hall. The famous W.E. Sangster was the speaker and Robert and his mates went along. The spacious hall and gallery were filled to bursting point every evening. The singing was thrilling, and the strange English accent of the great man of God made for compelling listening. Robert's pulse quickened as he listened night after night.

Though only eleven, he understood that the appeal to commit your life to Christ included him. He wasn't doing anything terribly wrong, but he knew his life had no focus apart from football. He began to walk forward; he had to be up at the front. He needed Christ in his heart, guiding his life. "*Lord Jesus, come into my heart,*" he prayed as he knelt. "*Come in today, come in to stay. Lord Jesus, come into my heart.*"

And Jesus did.

A long battle lay ahead of him as he built up his relationship with the Lord over the years. His next four years were spent at Linfield Secondary Intermediate School, which adjoined Blythe Street Primary. He tried to work steadily and well. He was working now for his Lord, and he made the "A" class each year.

Playing football for the Boys Brigade team was a big part of his life.

He was good, and his mates began to depend on him. He liked people depending on him. Even the Nicholsons had begun to depend on him a lot. One Saturday he sliced his knee badly on a very rough football pitch. Blood poured from his injury, and he was taken to a nearby hospital. The knee was duly stitched, and he was sent home. Within days, it was "swollen up like a bap." This time he went to a different hospital and was told the wound hadn't been cleaned properly before it was stitched. They removed some stitches and drained the puss.

Again, he was despatched home. Sitting on the sidelines during matches was not his style and he found it very hard to sit still, but the pain from his knee reminded him when he got too enthusiastic.

While watching the match a skirmish developed near him, he did not have time to get out of the way before four muddy bodies descended on him, all fighting for the ball. A stray foot caught him full on his injured knee. The whole wound split open and green puss flew in all directions. He rolled around on the ground in absolute agony, biting his lip hard. The wounded knee was more carefully tended to this time and healed quickly. Apart from his kneecap sitting at an odd angle and a nasty scar, he had no further trouble from it.

Meanwhile, Uncle Bob's health was deteriorating. He had suffered from leg ulcers for many years which drained his health. Finally, he died and was laid to rest in Belfast City Cemetery.

Elocution had given Robert a good speaking voice. He was losing his broad Belfast accent, saying "ing" instead of the usual "in" at the end of words, and many of his playmates didn't like it. They felt the voice indicated snobbery and they had no time for that. He had to stick a lot of teasing from the other kids and a certain unpopularity because of it.

Soon school days were over. With two letters of reference, he set off at fifteen to seek his fortune. He applied for a job advertised by a window blind company, but soon found he didn't like the work.

He moved on to a wholesale shirt manufacturer in King Street and settled in. He was given responsibility for cycling around Belfast on various errands and thoroughly enjoyed that. Meanwhile, he was playing football on Saturdays for Glenavon under eighteen's team.

One Saturday, he made sure his kit was spanking clean. He had new laces for his boots, he checked the studs to see if any needed replacing, and he even replaced last week's mud with some polish. The game was in full swing when he had sorted out who was who from the spectators. He knew the local Belfast team officials and by a process of elimination, was able to work out who the Sheffield Wednesday's selector was. He moved like lightning digging up the green turf as his feet pounded the pitch. He put everything he had into that game, and his team shirt was soaked with sweat. He leapt in the air punching it with his fist when he was offered a month's trial with Sheffield Wednesday's under-18 team. They would organise accommodation in "digs" for him in Sheffield and wanted his answer straight away.

Bobby, as he was known in footballing circles, was off like a shot on the first possible boat. His digs were in the home of Mr. Springit, the professional goalkeeper with the Sheffield Wednesday team. He could hardly contain his excitement as he walked into the stadium that first morning for training. He had met the other lads in the changing room. They were a motley bunch but seemed friendly. He was really going to work at this. This was now to be his whole life.

He soon found he had a lot of time on his hands. The other lads enjoyed going to the cinema, but Robert soon tired of their ideas of fun. Football was now a way of life for him, just what he had always wanted … or was it? Harry Catterick earmarked him for a good career in the English League but even that did not quell his doubts. Sheffield Wednesday offered him an amateur status contract, with a weight building programme built in because of his slight build.

However, he just wasn't happy. He began to think of his old friends back home and realised if he went back, he could still play football in the evenings and on weekends. Possibly this was the best thing to do.

As he was coming off the pitch one evening after an exhausting game, a man pushed a tract into his hand. He unrumpled it in the changing room. As he read it, he realised his life was no longer Christ-centred; football now occupied first place in his heart. Football was fun, but he was wasting his life on it. He could see that when he got to the big league and was of drinking age, it would all be "booze, girls and riotous living"! That finally made up his mind. He came home rather quieter and wiser than when he had gone away.

At home, he got a respectable job and signed up with Glenavon Football Club, travelling to Lurgan for training and games. Even this became tedious after a while and left little time for social activities.

He transferred to Distillery which was closer to home.

The Grosvenor Hall had a lively group of about thirty teenagers, most of whom attended the Friday night Youth Club, Sunday night after church Fellowship and Tuesday night Christian Endeavour. These friends and activities made a big difference to Robert. He had been verging on chucking in this whole Christianity business but instead he wisely chose the one that needed a certain amount of restraint and discipline. He knew that in the end this would give him lasting peace and fulfilment. He found the friendship of other young Christians who were struggling with the same issues very refreshing.

Wee Jimmy, as he called his foster dad, had had some difficulty keeping control over Robert. Like many teenagers, Robert regarded himself as the possessor of all knowledge. Wee Jimmy was merely four foot nothing (at least according to Robert) but he had muscles of iron from being a steel rivetter in the Belfast Shipyard. During one of these fracases, he grabbed Robert, at five foot nine, by the scruff of the neck, lifted him and held him clean off the ground and told him exactly what he thought of him. He was utterly humiliated and not anxious to ever repeat that experience. He came through the blind panic of his teenage years and had chosen a path that was leading him to a closer relationship with his Lord. Robert's life had turned a corner.

Wee Jimmy and Sadie had to be up early for Jimmy's shift at the shipyard, so they were always in bed by 10 p.m. Robert loved coming home to an empty kitchen and scullery where he would make himself some bacon butties with huge slices of white bread and a big pot of tea and would settle into an easy chair and just enjoy the quiet. This was the time of day he found it easiest to talk to God. He would place an empty chair in front of himself and begin to chat, telling Jesus about the day's happenings, asking forgiveness for his shortcomings, for the harsh word spoken in anger and the thoughtless deeds done in haste. A beautiful peace was taking over his life and he'd had a long chat with his boss and minister about his future.

One evening as he was praying in his quiet time, a strange awe gripped him. The whole house became still and silent as if a mighty hand were resting on it. The presence of God was all around. Robert covered his head with his hands and silently knelt, hardly daring to breathe in case he should disturb the stillness. For hours he remained motionless, drinking in the unspeakable joy that seemed to be all around. He finally arose, went to bed and slept like a baby. The next morning, the sky seemed a more radiant blue than ever. The birds sang more lustily as if they had been party to the previous night's experience. He dressed quickly, bounded down the narrow wooden staircase and threw his arms around Sadie, who shrank away in fright at his exuberance. He was into work early with a full understanding of where his future lay. His boss, a lovely Christian man, gave him all the support and encouragement he could. Rev Eric Gallagher, Robert's minister, was overjoyed at his decision to become a Methodist Minister. He would have to pass GCE "O" levels and local preacher exams to gain entrance to Edgehill Theological College, the Methodist training college for Ireland.

Night classes at Shaftesbury House School solved the first problem of the GCE exams. Finding the hard slog of study now quite enjoyable, he realised he had been a late starter and in fact could attain quite high marks. Local preacher's exams were the next hurdle. Greek and Hebrew were a new experience. Learning these languages took time and effort as whole new alphabets and vocabularies had to be learnt, but Robert was determined.

College was not grant-aided, so he would need extra money. Wee Jimmy and Sadie were very generous, but Robert felt a better job would help him save more. A position was advertised in the local press for a clerk in Ewart's Spinning Mill American department.

Robert applied and got the job. He was to take over from a chap called Ken, and they were given a few days together for Ken to show Robert the ropes. Robert was quick to learn, and they found that they had a lot in common to chat about. They quickly became firm friends and as Robert listened to Ken's animated conversation, he realised Ken had a God-given insight into the Bible that he found refreshing. As they talked, Ken leafed through a well-worn Phillips volume of the New Testament, explaining what the Lord had shown to him. The days passed quickly, but the friendship that had begun so unexpectedly was to last all his life.

Chapter 4

Confetti will have to wait

Ewart's Mill was completely different from anywhere else Robert had worked previously. Perhaps it was because he now had a real purpose and a worthwhile goal. He realised he had potential and was aware that his elocution and his music lessons had been in God's plan. This made him walk a little taller than before. His identity was emerging with his newfound confidence.

The corner where Sandy Row and Donegal Road met was not far from Hunter Street and was a favourite meeting place for the local layabouts. One sunny day Robert was walking when a well-known harmless creature accosted him and grabbed his arm, "Bradford, any odds?" He meant it would be wise to hand over any loose change.

Robert calmly reached into his pocket and gave him a handful of change.

"Is that it?" asked the man.

"That's it, Sammy." Robert walked away smiling.

Robert worked hard and by March 1964, he had finished his local preacher's exams and been accepted by the Methodist Church in Ireland to enter their ministerial training course in the next term.

The Methodist Conference decided that Robert's first year of training should be spent on circuit. He had to hastily acquire a black suit and clerical collar or two before he was off to the Tyrone/Fermanagh border, to a small town called Fivemiletown.

His departure day had almost arrived. He was walking down Sandy Row in his new gear, feeling a new sense of responsibility on his shoulders, along with his clerical collar and perhaps showing off just a little, when he was again accosted by Sammy. There was a marked difference in his attitude this time. He didn't grab Robert by the arm as before, or even block his way. He sidled up alongside him as he walked.

"Good day, Mr Bradford," he said, touching his cap respectfully.

"Mr. Bradford it is now?" Robert thought, chuckling inwardly and trying not to smile.

"Would it please your Reverence to help a poor fellow human being less fortunate than yourself, Sir?"

Robert, smiling broadly by now, handed him over the usual handful of change and went on his way chuckling loudly. He loved these working-class people.

"Salt of God's earth," he called them. "There is no time for nonsense in those homes," he would say, "no airs and graces."

For most folk, there was no escape. The street they spent their childhood in, was often where they spent their married life and where they died. Few ever had the chance that Robert was getting, and he not only knew it but was especially grateful for it.

"Fermanagh, here I come," he thought as he packed. He was off to be a "fisher of men." He knew he was fully in his Master's will, and the sense of peace that gave him was only superseded by his excitement about what lay ahead. Any tensions he felt, he bottled up as usual.

The traumatic effect of his early rejection had left him very insecure, but he pushed any fears to the back of his mind. He had to trust in the Lord. He was now stepping out in faith, in total dependence on a God who had never let him down.

Perhaps if the inhabitants of Fivemiletown had known a little about the human being that was about to be unleashed on them, they would have battened down the hatches and taken more notice.

Rev. Bolster took him to the farm where he was to stay and introduced him to the family. Robert instantly felt at home. It wasn't long before he had his shoes off and his feet planted firmly on the large Aga stove, enjoying its radiant heat. All sorts of goodies were produced, and Robert was introduced to a farmhouse fry as only country folk can make. The cosy farmhouse kitchen had a charm all of its own with its well-worn comfy chairs and sleeping mongrel dog. The aroma of freshly baked wheaten bread, the taste of warm frothy milk straight from the cow, a fry of griddle wheaten, soda bread, potato bread, fresh eggs and bacon were tastes he acquired a liking for remarkably quickly.

It took longer to get used to the pungent smell of farm animals in close proximity. The washed down concrete yards and hosed down milk byres, fields of ripening corn and barley rippling in the gentle breeze and winding bumpy lanes, leading from farm to farm, were in complete contrast to anything he had ever known on Hunter Street.

By 1966 Robert was back in Belfast at college and I was finishing school. Mods and Rockers were in their heyday, and they used to congregate around the City Hall. Donegal Square Methodist Church, which is situated right beside the City Hall, had a large basement which they opened as a coffee bar. Edgehill students used to come to chat to these teenagers. Robert took me with him on a few occasions.

There was snooker and table tennis, coffee tables and chairs, where discussions took place. We talked about Jesus Christ and about how knowing Him had given meaning and purpose to our lives.

Discussions developed on evolution and on whether Scripture was infallible. Could it all really have begun with Adam and Eve? I listened to Robert as he explained that Adam probably meant many men. I began to realize, as he did too, just how unconvincing these arguments were. My own thoughts on evolution at that time convicted me, and after a while we stopped going. We needed to get our own thinking sorted out before we could try to convince others. Bible truths were beginning to shine through the shallow, manmade theories with a crystal-clear light.

We spent every spare moment of that summer together. *The Sound of Music* had come to a Belfast cinema and Robert managed to get tickets. One beautiful hot summer day we parked our car in a narrow alley off Howard Street, near the city centre. I pushed my handbag under the front seat and Robert's coat was on the back concealing a brightly wrapped wedding gift. The film was spectacular and enjoyable apart from trying to wipe choc-ice off my white dress in the dark! We walked happily back to the car, only to discover that it had been broken into. The side vent had been forced and the contents of my handbag and Robert's coat pocket were strewn all over the floor.

Robert's Parker pen was still there and the tea set was still intact in its box. The only thing that seemed to be missing was the money in my purse.

"How much had you?" Robert asked.

"One and nine pence," I replied.

"Oh, that's not too bad", he said, breathing a sigh of relief.

I wasn't so relieved. That was all the money I had until the next pocket money day, but I certainly wasn't going to tell him that. We were both relieved that the car itself was still there, as it could easily have been stolen. We drove to Barnett's Park and unloaded our picnic from the boot, walking down the long, grassy slope of the park until we found a quiet corner near the trees to enjoy our picnic.

The lovely long summer days with picnics at the beach, evenings out to the cinema to see some epics, all made the days fly past. Robert would call at "Tara," our lovely seaside home set on a hill. He would stay for a meal and chat with Mum and Dad. Our spacious lounge was much used in the summer months with its beautiful view of the sea and parts Scotland on clear days from its enormous plate glass windows. Dad would lounge in his well-worn armchair, and Robert would make himself comfortable as together they set the world to rights, rarely agreeing on how that should be done. I steered clear of these discussions because I inevitably ended up getting cross with one or the other or both. Tea ready, we would pile into the dining room for salad, homemade wheaten bread, jam and cakes all prepared by my hard-working mother. The evening was then ours as we reversed out of the driveway on to the pot-holed lane and drove away. Robert would drive slowly, one hand on the steering wheel, the other clutching mine as we headed for one of our favourite beaches.

Robert crooned, "Catch a falling star and put it your pocket, save it for a rainy day" in a close imitation of Perry Como. The world was our oyster. I had many years of training ahead and so had Robert, but we felt as if we had all the time in the world. Those blissfully happy days became cherished memories for us.

College summer holidays were a time also to top up on funds for the year ahead, so Robert had taken on a job for "The Twelfth" fortnight, the annual July holiday, as a night watchman in Ewart's Spinning Mill. The factory had been broken into several times and the management thought it wise to employ extra guards over the holidays. Robert and three others took it in turn to walk the full round of the factory each hour. The walk took half an hour. The linen looms were only rested once a year, and the quiet night air was punctuated with the cracks and groans of wooden machinery contracting as it cooled. There were stations at various points around the factory that they checked into in order to ensure that the whole factory was covered each time. As the week progressed, Robert became more and more tired. Many days he got no sleep at all as he was helping out on the Newcastle circuit and had to visit the congregation during the day, as well as prepare sermons. The long nights consisted of telling jokes and ghost stories.

On the very last night of the fortnight, Robert drew the last walk.

By now totally exhausted, he was very relieved that the fortnight was almost over. He walked quickly as he neared the end. He could visualise his warm bed, his soft feather pillow with his head sinking into it as he pulled the covers over his shoulder. He just had to walk down the iron stairs into the boiler house, up the other side and he was home and dry. He opened the door and started down when he came to an abrupt halt. There in the middle of the floor lay a body.

Feeling it would be unwise to tackle this situation on his own, he ran to get the others. They roared with laughter at his distraught state.

"That's the boiler man," they cackled. "He's in to light up the boiler.

Then he lies flat on the warm floor and has a kip." It was a while before Robert was as amused as they were; he had been thoroughly shaken by the whole affair.

September saw about 40 of us girls from many different backgrounds landed into "The Beeches," a large house to accommodate us as we began our nursing training. It was like boarding school all over again, only worse. Just when I thought I was walking into adulthood, we were treated once again to lockup, rollcalls, uniforms and a strict time regime. I was fed up. I had expected to be treated more as an adult.

Once again, I had a curfew. I was sitting in Robert's car taking the best out of every second, then I walked wearily to the door just as the Matron in charge of us came out. She slammed the door deliberately right in my face! I was so shocked! I stood deliberating what to do.

Robert's car had disappeared out of the driveway! I went around the back up the fire escape and knocked on a bedroom window and got in. Rollcall was taken some time later and my name obviously was ticked as present; I was sent for. Standing in front of Matron she asked how I got in.

"Through the fire escape," I calmy answered.

I heard no more about it.

Dermot, my brother, was visiting one evening when girls came running and screaming. Dermot jumped to assist! A bat had got itself into a room, causing hysteria. He caught and released it outside and we all laughed with relief. It had been lovely of him to visit as I didn't see him very often, though I suspected 40 girls in the building might have had an influence on his thinking.

In his second year, Robert was elected as Chairman of the Students' Union. This meant that he had responsibility for organising the various preaching appointments, among other duties. It also meant taking the more inaccessible services himself. Consequently, he travelled to many of the farthest corners of the country and on Sundays, when my off duty allowed it, I travelled with him. Being Chairman, meant he had to try to keep the peace within the student body. But there were times when mischief overruled responsibility. One of the mature students had missed out on the cold bath initiation ceremony, as they were only required to live in for one week. Robert and some of the others decided to do something about this. They dismantled the man's bed, took out the light bulb, closed the door and with a piece of string, flicked the small bolt home so that the door was locked from the inside. In the darkness of Robert's room, they waited for what seemed like an eternity. There was the sound of heavy feet on the linoleum corridor and the rattling of a door handle. Then, a more insistent shaking of the stubborn door. Next, the sound of a solid shoulder being shoved against the door and the sound of feet walking away down the stairs. The friends contained their laughter until silence reigned, then exploded. Wondering what would happen next, they were soon put out of their misery as they heard Miss Thomas remonstrating with the gentleman.

"What do you need the axe for?"

"Just to break down my door."

Miss Thomas gasped, "You can't do that."

"Just watch me!" he exclaimed as he marched forcefully down the corridor and rounded the corner.

He took the blunt end to the door and the bolt gave way. Assuring the terrified housekeeper that he would pay for the damage, he flicked the light switch to no effect and threw the axe where the bed should have been. It hit the floor with a resounding thud. He turned on his heel and marched back down the corridor, shouting, "I'm going back home to my wife."

Miss Thomas went straight to Robert's door and knocked and tried the handle. Finding it locked and getting no answer, she went on her way. When all was quiet the boys replaced the lightbulb and reassembled the bed.

Robert was called to the principal's study next morning. Standing outside the door, he decided it was best to come clean and own up. He would probably be disciplined and lose his prized Chairman's position but the whole episode had been his idea. He stood guiltily in front of Mr. Greenwood who demanded to know who was responsible for the outrage. Robert opened his mouth to reply when the door opened and Miss Thomas burst in.

"There's no point in questioning Mr. Bradford," she said. "He'd been asleep in his room through the whole affair. I tried his door. You know how ill he has been."

Mr. Greenwood turned to Robert. "I want to know who is responsible for this. That bolt will have to be paid for."

"Yes Sir," said Robert, turning on his heel and walking out, scarcely able to believe his good fortune.

At times I remonstrated with Robert at what I felt was his irresponsibility.

"We are steeped in religiosity all day at lectures, then spend our weekends taking services. We live very close to God, but if we didn't let our hair down from time to time, we would go mad."

Making up our elaborate RVH nursing student headgear was a lesson all in itself. Our dresses had to cover our "popliteal" spaces (i.e., the pit at the back of our knees). Everything had to be pinned and buckled in very exact fashion. Needless to say, not all did, as we were teenage girls at heart, encountering medical students, some of whom were quite acceptable and unattached.

Being on the wards with actual patients was new, exciting and scary. We'd had six weeks preliminary training in the Beeches before being let loose on actual people. People's lives would be in our hands someday soon!

We transferred accommodation to Musson House in the hospital grounds, in later years to move to the more modern Bostock House next door.

Edgehill College was loosely affiliated with Queen's University. This meant that Robert could play football for the Queen's soccer team.

Having lost a lot of weight being ill with a stomach ulcer, he began to work towards full fitness again. An Inter University game was to be played on Stranmillis College playing fields at Shaw's bridge.

A brisk wind was blowing that crisp winter's day and there were some skiffs of rain as the spectators, including me, huddled together for warmth. The fast game was well under way on the soft ground when Robert performed a spectacular overhead scissor kick that resulted in a goal. I had been brought up on rugby, so soccer was new to me.

I had never seen anything quite like it before meeting Robert. I was awestruck. A little further on in the game, he tried again but it didn't come off.

"Should have known it wouldn't have come off twice, Bradford," mumbled his coach beside me, warming himself by slapping his hands against his body. It was hard to work up any excitement as I was numb with the bitter cold wind. I was frozen! The game was over.

Queens had won. I found myself swung off the ground and hugged by a muddy, half blind player who badly needed a shower.

As Chairman, Robert soon became fed up with accounting for everyone's movements and locking up at night. He came up with what he felt was the perfect solution and had twenty-four keys cut for the front door. At least students could let themselves in without resorting to climbing in through the dining room window. Inevitably, they would shake the table where the breakfast things were stacked up, making a fearful racket and, in turn, waking the Greenwood's noisy poodle.

As part of their training, students visited local prisons. Robert and the others, bedecked in their clerical outfits, were shown around. It was all light-hearted until Robert came face to face with an old friend.

John and Robert had been mates as teenagers, but while Robert had decided to follow the Christian path, John had chosen quite a different path and was now paying the price for the way of life he had chosen.

"There but for the grace of God, go I" really came home to Robert then. The magnitude of what the Lord had delivered him from shook him, and he uttered a heartfelt prayer of gratitude to the Almighty.

Another college year over, Robert was off to Cork for a few months.

There followed a searching period in his life. He took with him Sangster's book *Pure in Heart*, an essay on sanctification. "An essay which has cut through the repelling conceit of a self-sufficient young man," he wrote. How little he had to offer the Lord and yet God was using him. Robert wrote to me:

"As I walked tonight in the cold evening air a voice seemed to be continually saying to me, 'What are you?' As I tried to answer I began, 'I am someone who enjoys his work.' Yet the voice seemed to

say, 'That isn't what I asked you. You may know where you are going and enjoy the work, but—what are you?' Then the whole experience made sense, my love. Over the past few weeks, I had been made to face life as it is, not as I would like it to be, made to face myself as I am, not as I would like to think of myself—in short, I have been having an overdue dose of humility. You see, love, at the end of the day I am nothing more than a small part of God's universal vehicle of grace, with no promise of greatness, outstanding success, or even success at all. I can almost sense your reaction, here he goes trying to put me off again! Not this time, love, indeed the very opposite—while I realize I am simply what I am, whatever the future might hold, it will have to contend with not merely Robert Bradford, but him and also one on whom he relies greatly, namely my darling Norah. You not only complement the work that I do—your love for me and our mutual love for Christ is the very source of all I try to do."

The farming family that Robert was lodging with in Clonikilty, County Cork, shared his sense of humour. One day, Robert was travelling from the farm into Cork city when he heard an ominous rumbling sound every time he turned a corner. He slowed down and turned into the first garage he came across.

"I'm afraid it may be something serious. There's a fearful noise."

The car was put up on a hydraulic jack and carefully inspected underneath. Then the engine was checked out.

"Anything in the boot, Sir?" asked the mechanic in despair.

"Nothing!" replied Robert.

"Let's take a short trip and I will try to identify the noise," suggested the mechanic.

Off they went, and sure enough, on the first corner there was an ominous thud. Back at the garage, the mechanic asked Robert again if there was anything in the boot.

"Nothing but the spare wheel. I'll show you," said Robert as he opened the boot. There lay a very large boulder.

"Tom!" exclaimed Robert, in sudden realisation that the boulder had been put there by the son-in-law of the family.

The mechanic was highly amused. Robert went on his way planning his revenge on Tom.

Back in the north, he tackled a different job in Dobson's. His friend Jim Rea had been offered the job and couldn't take it. Robert stepped in knowing he would need the money. Making ice cream by the gallon seemed the perfect way to spend a few hot summer weeks, but by the end of his time there, Robert was heartily sick of the sight of it. He was greatly relieved when the job ended.

In my second year of nursing, there was more responsibility given and expected. "Specialling" an unconscious patient meant being alone with them for hours at a time, taking BP and pulse, etc., watching for change. Some were easy but at other times, they would be critical cases.

We were expected to spend six weeks in each department if possible during our training. I transferred to the main theatre block and found a niche I fitted into and loved. Soft of heart, I found casualty, where procedures we had to do often, caused extreme pain. It was a distressing experience, whereas in theatre, everyone was asleep and didn't feel a thing. I loved the thrill of it. I loved setting up the trays for the next operation, autoclaving and getting ready for the next case. My first stint was on nights with a "Sister" who was lovely to work with and encouraging to us all.

Only emergencies happened at night and sometimes we'd be sent to a ward to assist if they were short until we were needed for an operation. Day duty in theatre was even better, as open-heart surgery had recently begun in South Africa Groote Schuur Hospital under Dr. Christiaan Barnard. Encouraged by the new expertise, our own surgeons did amazing operations. I was permitted to watch ground-breaking procedures: heart valves being made from the patient's own thigh muscle performed by one surgeon, while another opened the chest cavity and prepared the heart to receive this.

One of our top surgeons had shared a flat with my brother Brian years before and teased me incessantly. There was lots of laughter.

About that time, a bunch of my friends and I were allowed to move to a nearby tower blocks of flats. There were four in ours, four in another some floors down and a single flat. We were the seventh floor and overlooked a greyhound track. Several parties followed, packing many into the lounge of our flat or my friends.

Before we knew it, we were pouring over the first draft of stations, and a month later the second draft, when we could finally see where Robert would be sent in June, as his college years were over. It was Cregagh Methodist Church, at least for the next year. This was a huge relief as he could have been sent anywhere in Ireland. Cregagh was situated on one of the main roads out of Belfast and was not more than five miles from the hospital where I was completing my nursing training.

In June 1969, the political situation in the province was hotting up. Agnes Street Methodist Church, situated on Shankill Road, was right in the centre of a very troubled area. Police reinforcements were called in to help curb the gang warfare that was breaking out on the streets.

Most evenings, angry abusive words would give way to stones and knives. Several young ministers would be on hand. Robert tried to strike up a rapport with these teenage boys. He memorised many of their names as this was helpful in an emergency. He watched their antics and spotted the ring leaders who often stayed safely under cover, egging others on to engage in violence. Petrol bombs and bullets then appeared on the scene and life on the frontline as peacemakers became dangerous. I feared for Robert's safety, half expecting to be called to Casualty to attend to his wounds along with all the other casualties that poured in from all areas.

Perhaps with the heightened tension and the loss of my father that same month, the links between us had begun to loosen. I and my friend went on holiday to Dartford near London and were introduced to the church youth group. I became friendly with an attractive young man, and I really enjoyed the fun.

I got a lovely letter from Robert telling me how much he missed me.

Maybe I should go away more often, I decided.

Robert had taken the Boys Brigade to their summer camp in Sligo.

> *"The boys and officers were very friendly,"* Robert wrote, *"The food is quite good, except there is no lettuce. I do miss you very much, though it will only be three days until we meet again. This sounds selfish, I know, but I hope you are missing me as much as I am you. If these days are a guide to the kind of things that will happen in Cregagh, we are going to have a great time … all my love and prayers.*
> *Yours lovingly*
> *Robert."*

Robert threw himself into the work at Cregagh with great enthusiasm. The superintendent minister gave him a list for visiting the congregation and he set about finding his way around the various streets and estates, getting to know the various families, and encouraging non church goers to venture out on Sundays. First, he got to know them as friends, then he appealed to them to honour him with their presence in his territory.

The young church team was having mixed success. During one of the games in the Ormeau Park, Robert had sliced his knee badly. Robert was transported to hospital where the knee was cleaned, stitched and bandaged. Then Robert was told he needed an anti-tetanus injection.

He absolutely refused to have the injection until a male nurse was found to administer it. I told him a female nurse would have been much gentler, but he assured me his trousers were not coming off in front of any female! The next few weeks were difficult for Robert as he couldn't drive. He got fed up waiting for people to deliver him to different places. I drove him when I was off duty, but his visits of the congregation was curtailed. He was finding it difficult to exercise patience.

"I want you to see this situation and tell me what you make of it," he told me one day as he collected me from the hospital. Robert cooked my tea, leaving the dirty dishes for Sadie, despite my objections and off we went in his car. The cold, dark winter's night made me shiver.

We travelled past the Ormeau Park and on down the Ravenhill Road.

Robert parked the car in a side street and knocked on a dingy door set into a blank wall. An unshaven, unkempt young man opened the door. We followed him up the bare wooden stairway and entered a room about twelve feet square. It smelt stale and unhealthy. There was a dishevelled bed at one side and a tatty curtain strung across the window. The floor was bare boards apart from one small piece of carpet. Chunks of crusty bread were strewn across the floor, probably thrown there by the toddler who was lying in the middle of the bed, a comforter in his mouth. The child's face was filthy and it was obvious his nappy had not been changed for a long time. The woman made no effort to bring us into the room but remained sitting on the bed ignoring us. I imagined she was probably embarrassed. The man, in his early thirties, was doing all the talking. He stood in front of the door, which wouldn't go quite back against the wall. Then I realised why the silver-tongued man was trying to keep us out of the room.

Through a crack in the door, I saw the back of a very large colour TV set. This man who hadn't any money for clothes or food and who was pleading with Robert for assistance from the "Poor Fund," was clearly not as desperate as he was making out. We left without making any promises.

"What did you make of that?" Robert asked when we were safely in the car.

"He's not as genuine as he pretends. Did you see that television behind the door?"

He came to church this morning with a real sob story and I fell for it.

He said he hadn't eaten for four days. I brought him home, cooked half a pound of sausages, a large tin of baked beans and some Smash and put it all in front of him with a pot of tea but he didn't seem to be that hungry and only picked at it. I still wasn't sure. Maybe if he hadn't eaten for four days, he genuinely couldn't eat. I took him to the Grosvenor Hall Mission. He was very reluctant to go but as he was in my car, he had no choice. He was instantly recognized as a con man who had been around every charity in the city. Robert still didn't want to write him off completely. If the chap was living on his wits trying to con money off churches and charities, he probably merited help. The child was obviously going to suffer if something wasn't done about the situation. Robert, always conscious of his own difficult start in life, involved Social Services, and the family was given food vouchers for the sake of the child.

"I value your insight and help to identify the con man rather than the genuinely needy," Robert told me. "No doubt we will meet plenty of both in our ministry."

It was August 1969, and I was on night duty in the "Skins" ward. The hospital had been emptied of everyone who could safely go home.

The Assistant Matrons took turns to grab a few winks of sleep in a side ward, but on the plus side I had very few patients. We were on the third floor, with windows facing Grosvenor Road. Riots were taking place and factories were being burnt down. Some of the patients that were well enough to be out of bed joined me in the office. With the lights off, we watched mobs careering around the side streets, attacking the police and army vehicles then hightailing it into several people's houses only to regroup behind, plan strategically and begin again. Tiny lights were sailing towards our windows. I was watching them, fascinated, until someone yelled, "Get down, nurse, those are tracer bullets!" I turned and ducked under the desk.

The hospital was bulging with casualties, police, army, terrorists and civilians, all together. How could we keep our forces safe in these situations? There were no buses in the area as many had been hijacked for barricades. So, when it was time to go home, I began walking the now deserted street into Belfast, to get home to Donaghadee. That's when reality arrived. This was no cartoon or film show. This was real and I was in grave danger walking this area.

Sadie and Jimmy Nicholson had moved out of town to a quiet, suburban housing estate some years earlier, but Aunt Liz still lived in Hunter Street. Tension was very high in that staunchly Protestant area that bordered on an equally staunch Irish Republican area, so

Robert set about trying to get her a rentable pensioner's bungalow out of town. But the Lord went ahead of him! A flat became vacant in a small pensioner's section of the estate where Sadie and Jimmy lived, not two minutes from their door. With the help of a lorry, Aunt Liz was moved out quickly for fear of squatters. Over the next few months our relationship was still very up and down, but we decided to get engaged. I was in a study block that week but had Saturday off. We arranged to call with Robert's brother-in-law in Armagh, as he was a jeweller. Getting into the car I was excited, until I spied his football kit.

"You can't possibly be planning to play football today!" I exclaimed, but Robert brushed it off, saying he couldn't tell the team he couldn't play as we wanted to keep the engagement a secret until Christmas. I will play while you take my car go and show your ring to your mum, then pick me up and we can tell my folks.

It was pouring rain in Armagh as we parked on a street nearby and ran into the shop. Billy, Robert's brother-in-law, was out back mending jewellery. Swinging up the steps on his crutches, he greeted us warmly.

Robert and he chatted for a while.

"She looks as if she'd be worth spending a bob or two on," Billy teased.

Finally, the trays of rings that were within Robert's price range were brought out and we set out to choose one. I eventually decided on a two-stone diamond twist. Robert approved and then feigned a faint when he heard the price. After, he chose a signet ring to suit his well-groomed square hands, Billy suggested engraving the ring straight away, but Robert had an aversion to his middle name Jonathan and only agreed after some persuasion to have all three initials included.

Travelling back to Belfast, we were both very contented, and I thought Robert looked happier than I had ever seen him.

Mum was happy with my news, but we decided to keep the official announcement to Christmas day when the family would be all together. But before we could make our announcement, Robert gave the game away by "forgetting" to take off his ring for church on Sunday.

I was annoyed that the news might get to my family on the Methodist bush telegraph system before we had a chance to tell them.

Presents started to pour in. By the time we had received a third clock from various organisations in Cregagh, we wondered if they might be hinting at his time keeping.

We set the wedding date for December 5, 1970, almost a whole year away. The Chapel of Unity at Methodist College was to be our venue because of its size and location. The memorial stained-glass window dedicated to my dad's memory was as close as I could get to having him at the ceremony. A nearby hotel was booked for the reception and a photographer arranged.

The Troubles were only beginning and mostly affected ghetto areas.

We did have an army jeep in one of the photographs, but that was as close as it got.

The stationing draft announced that Robert was to spend his first year after ordination in June at Suffolk. This was a new church extension project and an exciting first placement.

Situated on the Falls Road just past Andersonstown, it was right at a Protestant/Catholic interface, a very tense place to begin our ministry together. The Housing Executive had ill-advisedly joined up the two estates with adjoining roads; a great idea in normal circumstances but this was anything but normal.

A new church building was to be started and Robert regarded it as a gift from heaven. The manse was not the usual large, dark, draughty building we expected; it was a bright, modern, semi-detached house in a pleasant area only about a mile and a half from the church. July came and Robert had to say farewell to Cregagh. The final quarterly meeting of the leaders of the circuit was to take place in Glenburn Church. When Robert told me I was invited, I realised there was to be a gift presentation. He teasingly warned me not to take more than twenty minutes to reply, as there was a lot of business to get through.

My worst fears were realised. I assured him that he would be the one replying on behalf of both of us. In the event, I was given a lovely green coffee set and managed to address the large congregation with two sentences and a very red face, before leaving Robert to take over. He made a point of thanking the Nicholsons for all they had done for him, and we dedicated our lives together to God.

Wedding preparations were now well in hand. Finally, the invitations were sent out and wedding presents began to pour in. The flowers were ordered, the Chapel of Unity was booked, and the hotel hairdresser was secured.

Then it happened. I was standing in the church vestibule on my brother Brian's arm, when I realised that I had forgotten my bouquet.

I grabbed a bunch of chrysanthemums from a nearby vase. The stench that hit my nostrils was one that only people who have removed flowers from stagnant water will relate to. The green water was dripping all over my beautiful dress. At that point, I woke up in a cold sweat, thankful that it had only been a dream.

Suffolk's small congregation met in the local community hall, which also served as a bingo hall during the week. The white, low set hall which they had been using until recently was the site for the new building and was to be demolished. This tumble-down building which had housed services for many years had a special place in the hearts of many of the congregation. Its broken floors held memories of many happy days and its now empty fireplace had glowed with fires most weeks of the years gone by. The mice now had free run both above and below the floorboards.

Once I had recovered sufficiently from my appendectomy to attend services, it was easy for me to come up when I was off duty, and I attempted to clean the house and attend some meetings.

Robert gathered a nucleus of people around him and infused them with his enthusiasm. He reorganised and simplified the filing system and streamlined visiting into localities, taking a leaf out of Cregagh's book. Anything further than that had to wait in accordance with the advice of an older clergyman who warned him not to attempt to change anything until he had been there for a year and had a chance to see how things worked. This proved to be excellent advice.

Robert would come up with a new idea and put the seeds of it into a discussion. Often the others would come up with the desired idea themselves and worked much harder at it, since it was their own idea and they were not offended by Robert continually suggesting new things. The Suffolk folk were so friendly and accepted me so readily that I found my shyness fading.

The manse was already furnished so we didn't need much. Two rocking chairs, a fridge and a television, given as presents, were the only other things we needed. The church leaders' board informed us that if we went to Hoggs China shop, a certain amount of money was available to buy a dinner set. I was absolutely thrilled and set off with my mum to choose from the glittering galaxy of tableware on show.

How would I decide? Out of the corner of my eye I spied "Pastorale" a Royal Doulton design I had seen years before in a friend's house and had loved from that day. I ventured a look at the price and was amazed to discover it was cheaper than most of the others I was considering. The decision was made, and I went back to Upper Green to tell Robert what I had chosen.

A congregational social evening had been organised for the presentation. The Walsh Hall, a small wooden hall on stilts, had been gaily decorated for the occasion. There on display on the table at the top was not only the dinner set but a matching tea set, an electric kettle and an electric blanket. An evening of music was provided by the choir and visiting soloists. This small closely knit community was willing and anxious to welcome us both. As we were leaving, they showered us with confetti and rice. We both knew we were going to enjoy our time there.

The wedding day finally arrived,

Robert was leaving for the church from the manse in Upper Green.

The best man, Jim Rea, arrived in plenty of time for them to organise themselves. Robert had purchased a book for his friend to thank him for undertaking the best man's duties. Jim sat down with a mug of coffee and a packet of chocolate biscuits and began perusing the volume on his knee. A lengthy discussion ensued and they might never have been dressed in time but for the timely intervention of our next-door neighbour Kathleen Good.

"Aren't either of you going anywhere this morning?" she suggested.

The two hastily got dressed and managed to make it to the church before I did. They wore black narrow-legged suits, clerical collars and red carnations in their buttonholes. Their shoes were highly polished and their hair carefully moulded into place.

Our cars were late and when Brian phoned, they had the time of arrival as the time of collection. A substitute was sent but the heater in it was not working, and a rug had to be wrapped around me. I was so afraid of crushing my dress that I unwrapped it as soon as our journey to Belfast began. When we got to Bradshaw's Brae, the car was crawling along.

"What's the hold up?" my brother Brian enquired.

"Don't want to be early," the driver replied.

"I would prefer to go twice around the block when we get there," I said, afraid we might hit traffic jams.

We did and arrived ten minutes late. By the time photographs were taken and I was walking up the aisle, I was twenty minutes late. My future husband was standing by the communion rail as the wedding march from the "Sound of Music" rang out. He turned slightly as I drew level and, looking very strained, he gave me a weak smile.

"This guy isn't sure," I thought. "It's normal to be nervous," I rationalised. "He's had a lot to organise. He probably hasn't slept too well. Do I really know this man?" I wondered.

The ceremony seemed to be over very quickly, and we were in the vestry signing the register. Outside the church, cameras clicked and confetti flew everywhere. With Robert by my side, I was the happiest person in the world at that moment. Then we were off in a limousine to a blazing log fire at the hotel reception. The dry, brisk winter's day held for the photographs, with only a little drizzle as we finished.

The meal was excellent, and the people I had seated together seemed to be getting on well. As we were upstairs getting changed, my bridesmaid Barbara and I watched in delight as my brothers scoured the surrounding area in search of our getaway car. We were being driven away by a friend, so their search would be in vain. However, they managed to capture our suitcases. I just hoped the extra rice and confetti wouldn't make our baggage overweight. Finally, we escaped after a delightful but tricky dash to our car.

Chapter 5

House to House Fighting

Staying overnight in London gave us time to rid our luggage of the confetti and rice, and allowed us to set off on honeymoon without declaring our status to everyone. We boarded a Dan Air flight to Tunis, the capital of Tunisia. Neither of us had travelled much by plane and it was exciting, especially the scary thrill, as our enormous plane thrust forward at high speed along the runway, pushing us back into our seats. The humidity hit us as soon as we disembarked, and we sweltered in our heavy clothes in the coach travelling to the hotel.

What an impressive, white-arched entrance gate! The single-storey hotel had cool marble floors and air-conditioned lounges. We had a ground floor mini apartment, with bathroom, corridor and back access to a patio area. Breakfast was served in our room when we awoke. I'd never experienced so much luxury!

At meal times, we were seated at long tables with others on the tour.

We discovered quite quickly that there were two soups on the menu, but we were only served one no matter what we ordered—one at lunch and the other at dinner. Most main dishes were new to the majority of us; it was quite a fun experience.

Days passed leisurely in the winter heat of North Africa. We strolled the beaches and visited the quaint walled village of Hammamet and the local shops. The sharp contrast between the luxury villas set in the orange groves and the many emaciated beggars came as a shock to us.

Taxi drivers ruled the roads, driving down the centre with their hand on their horn, forcing pedestrians to jump out of the way.

Bargaining for souvenirs was immense fun. Shopkeepers plied us with little cups of thick, black, bitter coffee and pretended to be insulted by our offers so that we had to bargain until we reached a compromise.

This was far more fun than shopping at home.

Sitting on the soft sandy beach, a boy approached us with a basket of oranges, just in season. He quoted a crazy inflated price so Robert quoted an equally crazy price under their value. I shall always remember his feigned horror. "What is this?" he shouted with his few English phrases. We laughed and bargained.

A camel ride was a new experience for us. Traversing a dry viaduct ledge, the camels walked in line at their own pace. "Suss, harrig!" the herders yelled to quicken the pace, so Robert thought he'd try it. His camel took off at a pace with its legs flying, while Robert clung on to the saddle horn with his legs in the air, very close to the edge of the precipice!

All too soon it was time to come home.

As we stood at the door of 35 Upper Green, I waited until Robert unlocked the door, then just stood there expectantly.

Giving me that Robert look, he protested, "You can't mean it!" but I did and he had to set down the heavy suitcases and make a real meal of lifting me over the threshold in traditional style.

In February 1971, we had the stone laying ceremony at Suffolk for our new dual-purpose building. It all looked so small as we squelched through the mud to survey the progress to date. It was exciting seeing the building grow from week to week. The ceremony took place in the pouring rain in the square block, which was to become the entrance hall. The chosen hymn summed up our hopes and prayers:

Jesus where'er Thy people meet
There they behold Thy mercy seat;
Where'er they seek Thee Thou art found
And every place is hallowed ground

The short service ended with a prayer, "Grant O Lord that we may prepare to build Thee a House, so our hearts may be prepared to worship Thee worthily within it, through Jesus Christ our Lord."

Robert had a great sense of humour. Sometimes I woke in the small hours thinking I was in the middle of an earthquake, only to hear Robert laughing uproariously at some joke he'd been trying to hold in. Annoyingly, he soon got back to sleep, but I didn't.

The Twelfth of July had arrived. In times past a fun day out for everyone, but times had changed with the terrorism. Church members were bustling around from early morning in the "Field" where the Orange Order Parade was to hold its service. The "Field" was situated on the outskirts of Belfast at Finaghy close to Anderstown. Tension in the province was at an all-time high and so the Anderstown Road, a Republican/Catholic area was roped off at motorway bridge with police and army guarding the parade in case of attack. The day went well and we sold tea and sandwiches to the weary marchers and onlookers.

At the top of Lenadoon Avenue in Suffolk, the Housing Executive estate had been linked up with the Republican/Catholic Anderstown Estate. Consequently, there was an easy escape route for troublemakers.

Many Roman Catholic and Protestant families had lived happily side by side for years, but this changed as violence from the Roman Catholic side was matched by the Protestant Tartan gangs who were quick to retaliate. If windows were broken in houses in Suffolk, the same thing happened in Anderstown, and many peaceful people on both sides found themselves in the middle of a battleground. Living at the interface area of Suffolk on the outskirts of Belfast, with the evil ferocity coming against both communities, Robert began negotiating, totally illegally, with Catholic and Protestant families who'd lived happily in mixed communities only to find themselves at the frontline and on the wrong side of a community being quickly divided despite all local residents' efforts. The Troubles had come to their doors.

Robert talked to folks who were distraught. Their prized homes that they had lived in happily for 20, 30, maybe 40 years were now on the wrong side of this new divide. Robert went from family to family and where a home was beautifully established and garden resplendent, they did a straight swap. Of course, the Housing Executive couldn't legally sanction this activity, but they would quickly realise this worked on the ground. Instead of their houses being destroyed, toilets and baths pulled out and smashed, windows and doors broken, these decent homes and decent tenants could live on, and the Housing Executive would get the rent!

The Irish Republicans, backed by their terrorists, had been intimidating people from their rented homes, posting forms of "request to move" through their doors. Children were threatened, mounds of rubbish were dumped into gardens, and neighbours would suddenly move in the middle of the night. Empty homes would then give the terrorists more leverage. Snipers operated against the security forces in the area, being none too careful with their aim.

Night after night we were called out to comfort a family who was terrified. Sometimes Robert went alone if he felt it was too dangerous, and I stayed home and prayed. In August, an estimated 200 Protestant families fled in one night. The news was reporting more on the defence of the Republicans than of the attacks against the Protestant families. The families moved their furniture by van or by lorry or even on car roof racks. The Tartan gangs were organised to assist in an effort to keep the houses occupied, to stem the flow of the spearhead terrorist families set to occupy home by home. It was like a cancer encroaching down the hill, with Protestant families being pushed out one by one. A meeting was called in the community centre, and strong resolutions were passed with tough men vowing to stick it out to the last man. Across the Province, Protestants who stood up to the Republican agenda were named Loyalists. Yet our congregation lived in these homes in the midst of all this fear and turmoil.

In a meeting close to Robert, a woman lit up a cigarette and, intent on following proceedings, didn't shake the match out fully before replacing it in the matchbox. The whole box exploded. She screamed and threw it in the air. Within seconds the hall had emptied. Hard men first, followed by the women and children.

Recounting the incident to me, Robert roared with laughter, "I wish you had seen their sheepish faces when they realised what they had run from!"

It worried us though because people were obviously frightened for their lives. People in the area turned to us as Robert was known as "The Vicar" or "Mr. Vicar" and I was "Mrs. Vicar." Time and again we would arrive to quiet an angry mob and hear the comment, "It's OK. The vicar's here." He took people's confidence in him seriously and did everything in his power to calm every situation he was called to. He negotiated with police and army personnel, putting across the peoples' point of view and trying to inform new battalions of troops what was really going on. On one occasion, when an army colonel refused to listen, we had the ludicrous situation of a mob of several hundred descending down the hill towards Suffolk to burn Protestants out of their homes. The army was being instructed to guard the mob from the people who were defending their houses.

Now there's something not told.

Thankfully the police understood the situation and the flash point was avoided. Residents were extremely annoyed by the army's behaviour and often sought to take the law into their own hands.

Robert continually involved the local leaders in dialogue with the authorities so that they could see progress and avoid further conflict.

With the exodus of 60 Methodist families in one night, we began to think we would have the opening and closing ceremony of our new building in one day. Lenadoon Avenue was emptying from the top down, and we soon worked out their tactics. A spearhead force of about ten families took over each home that was vacated by a fleeing Protestant family, as they gradually worked their way down the hill.

No one wanted to be in the end house as it took the brunt of any attacks and therefore home after home was vacated, generally late at night so that neighbours they had vowed to support didn't see them leave.

Robert and many of the men in the area tried to hold these houses in a vain attempt to halt the extermination of Protestants from their homes. Each person took an empty house and took turns occupying it despite the torrential rain and cold. Like the rest of the men, Robert came home simply to wring out his soaking wet duffle coat and have a hot bath and some food before heading back out.

A certain gentleman in the area was a fount of information, but always at least two days after everyone else knew it. He was known to the locals as "M15" and spoke out of the corner of his mouth, presumably in case anyone overheard him. "M15," Robert and two other men were standing near the top of Lenadoon Avenue one day about noon.

The torrential rain had stopped, and the sun had appeared from behind the clouds. The army post opposite was in an empty house on the corner of Falcarragh Drive and Lenadoon Avenue. While the men stood chatting and "M15" divulged his latest information to them, a lorry sped down the hill, swung right into Falcarragh, and a terrorist with a machine gun popped up on the back of the lorry and riddled the army post with gun fire. The bullets ricocheted across the road to where the men were standing. All the men that were chatting dived for cover. One man dived straight through a plate glass window.

Another put his shoulder to the door, and Robert found himself in the hall. It was all over as quickly as it had started. "M15" was found flat on his back in the mud pleading with the Almighty about the state of his suit and apparently unconcerned about his near brush with death.

Travelling to work at the hospital was a slow business and often army checkpoints meant long delays. The quickest was via terrorist-dominated Anderstown and down the Falls Road. The army could not set up checkpoints there for fear of snipers hiding in one of the local houses. Instead, checkpoints were set up on all access roads to the area. As Suffolk and The Royal Victoria Hospital were at either ends of the same road, it was quicker to drive straight through.

One morning I became aware that traffic ahead of me had become so scarce that there was only one car ahead of me, none following and none approaching. I sensed trouble. Rounding a bend I saw a mob a hundred yards in front of me, yelling in delight as the lorry they had hijacked caught alight and a sheet of flames rose into the sky. The car in front had managed to do a hasty U-turn and was approaching me at speed. I swung our heavy green Triumph car around and sped after it. The area was deserted. Not a single soul was to be seen along the wide road. I raced homeward, scared to think what I might be running into in the mile or so I still had to travel. I had almost reached a roundabout. Coming up Kennedy way on the left was another mob. I put my foot to the floor, and in a split moment, I wondered if I should chance going the wrong way around the roundabout and face possible death from oncoming cars. Fortunately, I managed to screech around the roundabout just before the mob reached it. I got back home badly shaken and decided that a day off work was in order.

Sadly, this was becoming "the norm" in peoples' lives.

That was the start of a few difficult weeks. To the left of the church was a private housing development, occupied mostly by Catholics.

We used this road as a through road to Finaghy. Barricades appeared on all terrorist-controlled roads. We were driving through the estate and turned into that private development. Young boys had blocked the road, hiding their faces behind balaclavas or scarves. Robert drove straight at them and they jumped out of the way. They shouted and we realised that there was another group 50 yards ahead. I was frightened as we were trapped. They quickly blocked the road and the youths reached into the hedges for their concealed weapons. Robert rolled down his window and shouted to one of the boys as we screeched to a halt beside him.

"Just what do you think you're doing, Seamus?"

Fear registered in the youth's eyes.

"Didn't know it was you, Sir," not wanting to say Robert's name.

"Move the barrier. He's OK."

We drove on and I sank into the seat weak with relief, heart pounding.

Seamus attended our youth club from time to time with some of his friends. Robert managed to recognise him by hearing his voice.

Instead of fear, anger registered on Robert's face—anger that mere kids of twelve, thirteen and fourteen were being instructed in terrorism.

There was a lighter side to "The Troubles" in Suffolk thanks to the teenage Tartan Gangs. On sunny days, Republican terrorist supporters on the top of the hill would bring out their hi-fi equipment and play IRA songs at full blast. In retaliation, the Tartan boys brought out their pipe band and marched around playing "The Sash" and other loyalist songs.

As the weeks passed, the spearhead terrorist group forced their way down Lenadoon Avenue house by house. The residents were panic stricken. No one wanted to be the last house so as one family moved out, so did the next.

At long last, it was the night before our grand opening Service. Our new church completed, we took a final look around, touching the new furnishings with joy and pride as we went. The sanctuary was a semi-circle on the long wall of the sand-coloured, brick-faced rectangular building. The circular white pulpit with a black base was set to the side of centre by a magnificent stained-glass window depicting the cross. At Robert's suggestion, the architect had included a few portions of red glass to lighten the effect of the blue, whilst in the centre of the cross was a magnificent twelve-pointed star. The communion rail and table of beech and polished stainless steel sat on a rich blue carpet and gave a modern effect, toning perfectly with the wooden tongue and groove, sloping ceiling. The sanctuary portion could be closed off by two enormous concertina doors that folded out of the wall to leave a bare rectangular space with high windows that were unlikely to be damaged by games. Blue carpet rolled out for the aisles on Sundays, the stackable black padded chairs were very comfortable. The effect was astonishingly beautiful for such a simple building. The organ had a special trolley so it could be moved about as needed. The choir room which doubled in size with folding doors, the fitted kitchen, the storerooms, the vestry, ladies' and men's toilets were all finished to the highest standards. We were justly proud of it all.

The joyful opening was followed by a two-week mission called "Behold the Lamb of God." Salvation Army bands had been asked to help and Robert, like the Pied Piper, went around the estates asking people to attend. The bands then went to the church to help with the singing. It didn't surprise us that opposition arose in the form of squabbles breaking out in the church before the services even started, but we quickly prayed that peace would be restored. Many people, both young and old, came to faith at that time. At one service, the communion rail was packed with young people kneeling or standing several rows deep, committing or sometimes re-committing their lives to Christ. This mission proved to be a great foundation for our work there.

Activities for the winter began with real zest and enthusiasm. Boys Brigade, Girls Brigade, Youth Club, Women's department, prayer and Bible Study groups meant that the new building was well used. A women's coffee morning, which attracted many local pensioners, was a great success. I rose early before work and made a batch of scones for them.

However, families were still rapidly moving out of Suffolk. Snipers were now using the flats at the top of Lenadoon to take pot shots at the army or the odd shot into the Protestant community to instil fear.

Our ladies' Bible Study prayer groups were effective in binding the powers of darkness in the area with the result that no policeman or soldier lost their lives protecting us despite the fact that the area was at the very heart of the fighting for many years. Most of our services had to be conducted with army Saracens guarding the doors. At times we could hear soldiers' feet as they ran along our flat roof to escape the gunfire.

By this time, many local residents had banded together in what they called the UDA, The Ulster Defence Association. They armed themselves with axe handles, air rifles and some legally held shot guns. They were no match for the sophisticated weaponry of the Republican terrorists who had been building up their arms for the onslaught for some time.

A member of the Tartan gang overheard a woman in a shop complaining about how close the spearhead families were getting to her home halfway down Lenadoon Avenue. She was informed that there was an empty house in Mizen Gardens. Within minutes a lorry was despatched to collect her belongings, much to the surprise of her husband who continued watching television while the gang cleared furniture and fixtures from around him. The gang took off with his furniture leaving the man to walk down the hill to his new abode in Mizen Gardens! Only in Suffolk would something like this happen.

Life was becoming increasingly difficult for older people, many of whom were afraid to leave their homes. The pensioner's bungalows were located at the bottom of a grassy hill and were in the direct line of sniper fire. Young people from the church began to go for their shopping and run errands for them.

Our church building with its glowing neon, stainless steel cross, shining like a beacon, became a symbol of hope for many people—but not for the terrorists. A group of us were standing chatting outside the church one evening paying little heed to the crackling of gun fire in the distance. I turned around to find everyone lying on their faces on the ground and yelling at me to get down too. The tiny sparks we had noticed were tracer bullets and had been just above our heads.

Later we saw the bullet marks on the wall, inches above where we had been standing.

Since the beginning of "The Troubles," barricades had appeared all over Northern Ireland. Cars, vans, buses and lorries were hijacked and often set on fire, their burnt-out wreckages used to seal off roads.

Bus companies and taxi firms tried to keep a service going to make life as normal as possible for people but often at a colossal cost. Many small businesses found themselves in "no-man's land" and were unable to get supplies in or merchandise out to their clients. Many were bankrupted.

One Sunday, the army set up a barricade of Saracens at the bottom of Lenadoon Avenue, completely blocking access to the street. Soldiers lined up facing the hill to ward off a mob of several thousand that was gathering to take over Suffolk. There were very few soldiers compared to the mob. That drizzly Sunday afternoon, the whole of Suffolk waited in suspense. The mob started to move down the hill using a lorry load of furniture as a battering ram. The Saracens pushed them back, and they retaliated with snipers until dusk.

The men, fathers and husbands were behind their own back doors with pick handles or whatever came to hand. As the battle raged, our women congregated in the church at the evening service time. We gathered in a circle and sang a hymn, then started to pray. Robert walked in quietly, anxiety written all over his face. He sat down beside me and just drank in the atmosphere. Refreshed by God's presence, he quietly went out again to join the army on the front line. The army won the day and the mob dispersed. Our dejected, frightened people went back to their homes, wondering what was to become of them in the days and nights ahead.

As I was frequently alone in the manse, I insisted we get a dog. At least that was my excuse. That's how Towser, a tiny scrap of a Yorkshire terrier pup, became part of our household.

Twinbrook Housing Executive Estate, further out of town towards Lisburn, was growing in size and several displaced families from Suffolk had been rehoused there. The streets were named after trees, flowers or shrubs. Azalea Gardens and Juniper Walk made for a very pleasant environment. A group of three huts were located in the centre of the estate for use by the community. The Catholic Church, a Community Centre, and Protestant denominations shared one of these. This worked very well—Protestants and Catholics living side by side in a fifty-fifty estate—until an influx of 130 Republicans squatters arrived overnight. All the residents banded together to try to stem the flow but were warned they could not block the roads, and the squatting continued. The small congregation that Robert had so carefully nurtured found themselves outnumbered two-to-one, and started to look elsewhere for accommodations once again.

By this time, both Robert and I had adapted well to married life, even if I had to play helpless at times when nagging didn't work.

I usually got home from work first as Robert walked to and from Suffolk as he liked the exercise. Most church members lived within a mile radius of the church and Robert felt the exercise kept him fit.

Arriving home just before him, I managed to be in the process of supposedly attempting to light the fire when he arrived. Before long, he assumed the duty of fire lighting while I prepared the meal. His fierce independence was difficult to cope with at times, but he was learning to include me in decisions.

As in any community, there were marriages that were going through times of crisis and, often, our spare room was needed by a family in distress. On one occasion a mother had to go into the hospital, and her little girl was going to have to go to stay with relatives on the other side of town, where it would not have been easy for her father to see to her. Robert came in one evening and discussed the situation with me. I immediately said she could come and stay with us. Robert was delighted as he had already suggested this to the mother. Many times, I found myself in that situation. I learned to keep beds made up and ready for an unexpected guest.

We loved having that little girl stay with us. It taught me more about the man I had married too. This apparently tough man, who was such a disciplinarian, was a real softy as far as little girls were concerned.

As his birthday grew near, Joanne and I had great fun planning our surprise. I baked a lemon sponge and she helped me decorate it with bright green icing. Then we piped white lines for a football field. She sorted out red and blue jelly babies for football teams, eating the spare ones. We even made goals with match boxes covered in royal icing and a football. It was lovely having a child around the house. It was becoming painful for us as we had no children of our own as yet. A sadistic birthday party followed where we tried to decide if jelly babies should be eaten head first or gobbled up from the feet.

Chapter 6

Families are forced to move out

Robert refused to wear a watch, relying instead on his memory. He was training his memory to do time keeping, he claimed. He also trained himself to remember peoples' names, feeling that it made them feel cared for if he made the effort to remember them and their families.

Towser, who had been bought to keep me company, became more and more Robert's dog. The church caretaker Alex and he were great friends. So, while Robert counselled or wrote sermons in the vestry, Alex and Towser would play with an enormous brush while Alex swept the hall. The racket of Towser's barking and Alex's laughter could be quite deafening at times, but Robert didn't seem to notice.

A perky little dog, he defended his home and family with fearless determination, taking on all visitors to the back door as foes. Visitors to the front door were spared this rowdy welcome. He was a dog with giant spirits despite his tiny size.

At the beginning of the week, Robert would start working on his sermon and write down whatever ideas came to him the rest of the week. While tensions were rising in our area, he did not have a minute to sit down for days on end. Each week, he still managed to preach a great sermon. He usually asked me for my views on the way home from church. I gladly encouraged him or gently told him what I thought might be helpful, as I knew how much work he put into it. One Sunday, after another difficult week in Suffolk, he asked the usual question. I reluctantly told him I thought the sermon was rubbish. Robert got the message and knew he had to re-evaluate his priorities.

With Joanne reunited with her mum, we set off on a short break to Wales, visiting his brother Don, Vera and son Austin. On the return boat from Holyhead to Dun Loaghaire, we met some friends.

"We are so sorry to hear about your church."

"Our church?" we asked in alarm.

"It was on the news. Apparently, it was blown up!"

We were in Dublin before we were able to phone and find out what had really happened. It was the wooden "Welsh" Hall of the church that had been destroyed, not the new building. When we heard no one had been hurt, we were greatly relieved. The papers reported the incident like this:

> *"The main shooting was in the Suffolk area where, from mid-day yesterday until early today, five hundred shots were fired at troops in the army post at Lenadoon, the main target. In the same area residents foiled two attempts to burn down a Methodist Church Hall at the Stewartstown Road. The first attempt was at 5pm when residents found a five-gallon drum of petrol at the rear of the building. Two hours later two men and a woman were seen near the building and a shot was heard. When local people went to the scene, the men and girl left on foot, one of them carrying a rifle and it was discovered that the lock on the door had been broken. A second drum of petrol was found at the scene."*

They finally succeeded in blowing it up the next morning. As no windows of the new building faced that direction, there was little damage to the church itself.

The "Vanguard" party had appeared on the scene on July 21, 1972, and a press release regarding the Secretary of State William Whitelaw's talks with the IRA was issued:

"The IRA leaders should have been arrested and brought to trial when they set foot in England."

The English Methodist Peace Fellowship was reported in the press as having passed a resolution supporting William Whitelaw and also saying:

"We welcome the promise of the introduction of proportional representation and assure him of the Methodist Conference's continued support."

Robert blazed with anger at these Englishmen who had no understanding of the problems we were living under. They were prepared for us to have to vote under a system they would not accept themselves. There was no comprehension of how we were living in fear of our lives and homes every minute of the day. They did not have to live as we did with distressed people calling at all hours. They did not live as we did, peering out from a darkened room to check if we could see the hands of the callers. If their hands were visible and empty, it was probably safe to open the door. If their hands were in their pockets or inside their coats, you had to be extra vigilant in case they were carrying a weapon. We offered a prayer for our safety as we opened the door, for open we did no matter what our fears.

Some English Methodist ministers came over for a short time to see the situation for themselves and went home enlightened about the realities of living under such constant danger and threat.

The Republicans/Sinn Fein focused on a media propaganda war seeking a backlash from Protestants. It was not that they cared even for their own community—you only need to ask the Catholic families that have an empty chair sitting in their home or search the bogs in the Republic of Ireland. It was because they wanted a United Ireland at any price, even spilling the blood of over "400 *innocent Catholics,*" as reported in *The Irish Times*.[2]

The Irish Republicans' hatred against anyone who was loyalist, or sought to unify dividing communities, became more evil in the 1970s, when they projected to the world that they were being persecuted, while in fact they had become the actual persecutors.

The terrorists knew that every shot fired into the Protestant community was a shot of fear into our minds, and if they shot someone, they would claim that they were not the intended target.

The police advised Robert to attain a permit for a legally held firearm, of which he purchased a gun. The problem was that he couldn't reconcile it with the thought of taking someone's life, so it ended up mostly in the house.

One evening, Robert came home and announced that some Roman Catholics wanted to come to our Bible Study and that he had told them they would be very welcome. I was concerned about how our church members might feel. Robert assured me that the congregation was not anti-Catholic. About ten people came faithfully for the next six months, walking through a treacherous area, until their families eventually persuaded them of the dangers of going into our area in the dark nights. Many interesting discussions took place as no passage of Scripture was avoided, and differing views were openly discussed. A new group of soldiers arrived in Suffolk. The majors and lieutenants were briefed:

---

2 Irish Times (October 7, 2021)

"Get to know the IRA Commander, the UDA Commander and Rev Robert Bradford and if you gain the confidence of these three, you will have a fair idea of what is going on in the area."

One night, we heard the noise of boots on the floor and turned around to see what was going on. A young, enthusiastic Lieutenant decided to come to church, and he brought his squad along too. A row of very uncomfortable soldiers marched in to occupy the back seats every Sunday, rifles lined along the back wall. They fidgeted as Robert preached a clear gospel message. A friendship blossomed with Lieutenant Cliff Burrage, although we were very conscious of why he was there.

After one evening service, Cliff followed Robert into the vestry to tell him of his dramatic conversion earlier that week. He explained how he had moved from a position of self-sufficiency to a realisation of his need of God's help. He had stepped off the pavement at Horn Drive and, while patrolling, had committed his life to God, stepping onto the opposite pavement as a new believer—a totally new creation.

In August 1971, about 500 Protestant families had found it necessary to move out of the area west of Stewartstown Road in Suffolk. This left only about 100 Protestant families still living on the Lenadoon side of the road. Around 22 buildings, comprising of houses and flats in the Horn Drive and Doon Road area had been left vacant and acted as a buffer zone for about six months. The decision had been taken to allocate these properties to Catholic families on the emergency housing list. The Suffolk Tenants Association wrote to the Secretary of State asking that some Protestant families be considered for these houses to help stem a further exodus of the few remaining families from the area. Robert was now playing an active role in writing letters on behalf of the residents to Members of Parliament or other government officials. The continuing intimidation of people was growing more serious by the day. The threats, rattling of bin lids, whistle blowing both day and night and window breaking was keeping everyone's nerves on edge.

Being involved with the new Vanguard Party, Robert decided that the best way of helping the situation was to stand for the Northern Ireland Assembly elections in June 1973. He was convinced he could do more as an elected representative, but it was not to be. The two long weeks of campaigning in South Antrim left us feeling optimistic, but because of the new proportional representation system of voting, he was eliminated on the fourteenth count. One lady claimed that she had put twelve votes against Robert's name, failing to understand, as did many others, that voting was in order of preference and that she should have put "one" against his name. So many people were confused by this new system.

The defeat was a real blow to Robert as he had entertained such high hopes. The posters on lamp posts and walls continued to flutter in our faces for many months, turning a knife in the wound of humiliation.

Through it, he learned humility.

My Daily Light reading on 30th June summed up our feelings:
"Humble yourselves therefore under the mighty hand of God, that he may exalt you in due time."

As the months passed, more and more people were coming to the services. The evening service was more popular than the morning service and provided a great opportunity for good teaching, to build people up in their faith. Redemption songbooks were purchased, and the choir sang gospel anthems as more and more people came forward to dedicate their lives to God's service.

Although mezzo soprano, I was called to sing alto to fill a gap in the choir. We sang some amazing pieces and became quite accomplished.

First Robert taught us, then Val Campbell, and then Beryl Hanvey, who played organ and led the choir.

"Politics wasn't the way," he said one evening as he sat at the piano playing his favourite hymns. I was standing behind him, my hands on his shoulders as usual, singing along with him, his tenor voice singing the melody and I the alto. Without warning he would change to sing the tenor line and I would laugh and sing the melody. We loved those close times when we could shut the world out.

In October with inter-church talks underway with the Roman Catholic Church, Robert launched his *Methodists Awake* campaign.

He put large advertisements in the press.

"Methodists Awake To The Dangers...

Of dialogue with Roman Apostates:

Of neglecting Biblical/ Wesleyan Fundamentals:

Personal or congregational letters of support for a rejection of unbiblical ecumenism will be gratefully received."

The press picked it up and in an interview in the Belfast Telegraph in September, Robert stated:
"I believe I am speaking for thousands of grass root Methodists who have NOT been consulted about these talks. A referendum of each congregation should be taken. My aim is to get the voice of ordinary Methodists heard at the next conference. I am not opposed to talks with Roman Catholics on social issues like drug abuse but talking to them on other issues is futile. The dogmatic stance of the Catholic hierarchy can never be altered. I believe that talking to Roman Catholics at the home level on theology is acceptable, for I feel a genuine concern that the grass root Catholic is being deluded and misled by the church hierarchy."

Determined to try to change our church from within he added:

"I am fighting to save the Methodist Church as laid down by our documents of faith, it is the Talk Supporters who have strayed from the official position."

A series of letters appeared in the press, both supportive and abusive, letters to us personally again supportive and abusive. A real campaign of bitter phone calls began, often leaving me weak and weeping or just plain angry. But the tremendous response from the Methodist people themselves made Robert press on.

The terrorists stepped up their campaign in Suffolk, and life on the estate was lived in a high state of tension. It is not possible to live normally during a terrorist war but the people tried. The army was always about the area, hiding here or there. If you jumped over a garden fence, you might have found yourself tripping over the prone form of a soldier on watch, the rest of the patrol around various corners and under hedges nearby. As you drove around at night and an army patrol came into your headlights, you turned them off and drove by sidelights for fear of them being picked off by the ever-present snipers.

The Republican movement goal was and is to wipe out the Protestant religion in Northern Ireland, as they have almost done in the Republic of Ireland. Due to this, they sought to burn or destroy anything Protestant including our churches.

The Church leaders wrote the following to the Secretary of State:

"May we stress once again the fears of our people, for we believe that the attacks on our church have been designed to undermine the confidence of our people, and thereby make them lose hope for the future? If this happens, it may well be that we will have another exodus of Protestant people from the area and we believe this is what the IRA wants."

It was a constant struggle to live normally despite severe intimidation, with windows being constantly broken, bomb scares where women would spend hours standing in the street unable to get home or pick their children up from school as it was evacuated. Add to that the worry of them being caught up in violence at an early age because of the environment in which we lived, we felt more than ever that the Lord had sent us to this area. We didn't have to go overseas to fight for rights and justice in a heathen land; we had all that in Suffolk. This was our mission field. But changed days were ahead.

Chapter 7

Robert becomes an MP

Early in 1974, our Yorkie bitch Boo gave birth to a litter of pups. I loved looking after these fluff balls before they were sold. Our house was filled with the sound of yelping puppies and for the first time, our home seemed full. In time, they were all sold and gone. I decided to go back to work in Musgrave Park Orthopaedic Theatre, a whole new sphere for me.

When I wasn't working, I was receiving anyone who was calling on Robert, and one Monday, a deputation arrived. I showed them into the sitting room and offered to bring them coffee, then I fetched Robert from his sermon preparation in his upstairs study.

When they left, Robert hastily told me, "They wanted me to stand as an anti-Sunningdale candidate in the forthcoming parliamentary elections." I glanced at him, rather apprehensive. "Don't worry. I told them I wasn't even slightly interested," he said.

Then he frowned. "They are coming back on Friday."

"What for?" I asked.

"They think I'll change my mind." He smiled.

"Will you?"

"No."

Each day that passed, Robert was becoming more and more anxious. By Thursday he was like a caged lion.

"What's wrong?" I finally asked in exasperation.

At this time, he was reading a book by Derek Bingham, *Amidst Alien Corn,* a study of the book of Ruth.

The greatest guiding line to follow when faced with a decision as a Christian is to shut your door. Get the influences of life out of your way and explain everything in secret to your heavenly Father by acknowledging Him. Then go and act in a common-sense like manner according to your abilities and limitations. When you acknowledge Him, He then directs your paths. Ask two simple questions: "Is it right? And is it necessary?" If there is no cloud between you and your Lord, go ahead.

Robert had acknowledged the Lord and it was only if it was God's will that he was prepared to take on this task. Was it right? He felt it was right to give people the chance to vote to show their disapproval of what the elected representatives were doing. Was it necessary for him?

The other three candidates had agreed that they would stand down if Robert was prepared to stand. This was an unheard-of precedent in politics. Yet, Robert still wasn't fully convinced.

The delegation called again and were met by a very subdued Robert.

"I can't say 'yes' but neither can I give you a definite 'no.' When do you need a definite answer?

Saturday night was the deadline. A meeting of candidates was to be held in Bill Craig's house and they would need his answer by then.

He walked down the stairs on Friday looking quite smug.

"Come to a decision?" I ventured from the kitchen.

"I've done something I have never done before and will probably never do again. I've put a fleece down."

"Pardon?" I asked, more than a little surprised.

"I've put a fleece down. You know the story of Gideon.[3]"

"I know what a fleece is," I interrupted impatiently.

"Well, it suddenly struck me that it costs a lot of money to fight an election campaign and as we are permanently in the red at the bank, we can't provide the funds. So I've asked God to provide the £1,000 we will need if he wants me to stand."

He was still smiling when the telephone rang beside him in the hall. His end of the conversation was monosyllabic, but his face was drained of all colour. I put the kettle on as he listened on the phone.

He replaced the receiver and went into the dining room. I found him hunched in a rocking chair staring into the blazing fire. I handed him a mug of coffee.

"Bad news?"

"That was a call to tell me that an anonymous gentleman has offered to back me to the tune of £1,000 if I'm prepared to stand."

---

3 Judges 6

Now it was my turn to sit down quickly. We sat in silence for some time letting the significance of it all sink in. Then Robert began to think out loud.

"If I stand and lose, there's the humiliation, even though I'm prepared for it. If by some strange quirk we won, then where would I be? Would we have to leave Suffolk? Could I do both jobs? The church would suffer because I wouldn't be able to spend anything like the same time on visitation. I would be in London for most of the week. But if that's how I am being led by God, then I must follow. Everything is going well in the church just now, and I can't believe it's all about to change."

Robert was like a stranger prowling around the house for the next 24 hours. He wanted me to accompany him to Bill Craig's house. That night as he drove, there was a complete silence in the car between us. When we arrived, we sat in the car in the driveway as he was apprehensive and still undecided.

He asked, "What do you think?"

"The fleece was answered fully," I said.

"I know, but I don't want it," he responded.

He slowly opened the car door and went into the house while I grew progressively colder as I stayed in the car and prayed for him, "Lord have your way."

Inside, the men were gathering around the dining room table. Then came the inevitable question:
"Will you do it?"

No one heard the answer as the chandelier above their heads gave a loud crack at that precise moment and everyone looked up. It seemed like a clear divine intervention!

"Yes!" Robert meekly replied.

The group was jubilant and began planning in earnest. Robert was still apprehensive and wondered what the people in Suffolk would think, but he shouldn't have worried.

The United Ulster Unionist Council or UUUC was a combination of Harry West's Unionists and William Craig's Vanguard Unionists and Ian Paisley's Democratic Unionists. They banded together as UUUC to give a united anti-Sunningdale platform for the election, and the battle was on for real. The printer worked night and day to produce leaflets and posters for the campaign. Raymond Jordan, who became Robert's election agent, worked from midnight until morning, producing the goods for his home bakery and spent the day organising the campaign without any sleep. Finally, the leaflets arrived.

ROBERT BRADFORD X {FOR SOUTH BELFAST}
UNITY WITH GREAT BRITAIN
UNITY OF ALL TRADITIONAL UNIONISTS
UNITY FOR THE DEFEAT OF VIOLENCE
UNITY AGAINST THE COUNCIL OF IRELAND.

The Belfast Telegraph on 20th June read:

"POUNDER SET TO MAKE IT A FIVE TIMER"

The paper gave a synopsis of the five candidates with photos and an article about how Mr. Pounder, the sitting candidate, would easily win again. With just eight days to go, tension was mounting. We knocked on every door in the constituency and handed in leaflets, except in staunch Republican areas, where our lives would be in danger. Teams of people gathered every night with carloads of literature and took off on foot to pre-arranged areas. Tramping the streets in dark, cold February was not pleasant, but as more and more people said they would vote for us, our hopes began to rise. I even lobbied some of the staff at Musgrave Park. The big breakthrough came one night when Bill Craig allowed Robert to take his place on a TV debate amongst the candidates. As we knocked on doors that night, we asked people to watch and judge for themselves, and they were obviously impressed with Robert's ability to speak his mind clearly and concisely.

He was sure of his facts, articulate and polite to his opponents, and immaculate in appearance.

As Thursday February 28, drew near, we began to get really excited with the tremendous reaction to our canvassing all through South Belfast. At our late-night gatherings in the Jordan's home, we began to feel we really had a chance of not just gaining the anti-Sunningdale vote, but actually winning the seat.

As I tramped the streets night after night, listening to the snippets of conversation from various groups of people, I found myself in a different world. I began to realise what a sheltered life I had led up until then. I hadn't realised how many people had refrained from swearing in my presence or how much the conversation had been toned down for my benefit, such was their respect for nurses and the Minister's wife. The shattering experience of knocking on doors and being sworn at, having doors slammed in my face or threats of having dogs set on me, were all new to me. The groups were very protective of me, but it was impossible to judge by the look of a house what kind of reception might await you there.

The voting day arrived and Robert and Raymond had a detailed plan organised to cover all polling stations. The phones were manned constantly, and they buzzed all day with people needing help of various kinds. Cars with loudspeakers toured the area, encouraging people to come out and vote in areas where we were concerned we might get a low turnout. In one area, Robert set up an account with a local shop to feed any of our workers who came in, and packets of sandwiches were distributed to various people at the polling stations, along with flasks of coffee. Standing at one of these locations, I was very grateful for this as it was bitterly cold. I offered coffee to my opponent, an Alliance Party worker giving out leaflets. She looked at me in amazement and cautiously accepted it. Did she really think I was going to poison her?

Finally, polling stations were to close, and Robert designated me as his representative to watch that the boxes were sealed properly. I noticed that one of the boxes was being left quite loose and I pointed this out.

"It might be to your advantage," the man whispered, looking around cautiously.

I was furious. I simply could not understand the attitude that anything goes. It was plain wrong!

"All's fair in love and war," he quoted, "and this is definitely war."

Few of the team had much sleep in the last ten days as we sat up each evening going over the day's events. Funny incidents were recounted again and again as each new group arrived and they added theirs. Tonight was the count, and one of our workers in Finaghy had become so confident of victory, that instead of handing out leaflets with Robert's picture and a short synopsis of what he was standing for, he was heard saying, "Get your souvenir picture of the winner here; get your picture of your new MP now!"

"Win or lose, it's all in God's hands," Robert commented on the way home. "But if I've won, it's going to change our lives drastically."

We had talked this over a little during the past ten days but now that the results seemed certain, we both felt apprehensive.

"The hierarchy of the Methodist Church aren't going to like it," I suggested.

"Well, we've got Lord Soper in the English Church in Parliament, so they'll just have to come to terms with it."

Raymond and Billy McAllister had been down at the count in the City Hall right as soon as they were allowed in. At nine o'clock they phoned us, just as we were getting ready to leave home. "We really think you will make it." They were very excited.

"They've opened some of the boxes from Catholic areas and you are getting an amazing number of their votes."

Robert went and finished shaving, singing lustily, then he ducked his head under the cold water tap as was his habit and dragged his hair flat before carefully encouraging each wave into place. I was ready long before him and waited impatiently.

"We'll be sitting there for hours, love," he smiled at me as he finally made it to the car.

The City Hall is an impressive building but that day I noticed little of it. We tried to look unconcerned as we walked up the white marble staircase and its long interminable corridors. The noise of voices was deafening as we entered the hall where the South Belfast count was underway. The people counting were seated on the inside of two sets of long tables facing out to the front and side of the platform. The first workers sorted votes into piles for pigeonholes with the various candidates' names on them. The next lot were counting them again in case of mistakes, and the rest were doing the final counting. The whole procedure was being carefully scrutinised by various candidates and their agents. The efficiency of it all struck me straight away. On the centre table were the finished piles of voting papers carefully elasticated together in piles of one thousand. At this stage the race between Rafton Pounder and Robert was neck and neck. As different boxes were opened, Rafton Ponder would race ahead by 1,000, then we would gain 2,000, then he would catch up again. As the hours ticked by and we increased our lead, the tension was palpable. A strained cordiality broke out between the candidates now that the battle was almost over. It was almost noon when Rafton Pounder came over and shook Robert's hand.

"I think you've made it. Congratulations."

What a gentleman, I thought. *But have we really won? Could it be possible?*

The hush had gone, the tables were being moved, and everyone was chattering excitedly. I found myself being pushed to the front beside Robert. The press arch lights were trained on the Presiding Officer who had a microphone in his hand, and the TV cameras were turning. His voice boomed out with the results in alphabetical order: Robert Bradford—22,083. A yell of delight went up and quickly stilled. Rafton Pounder—18,085. I thought the roof was going to lift off! Silence was called for and he continued with the rest of the results. Robert then spoke expressing his thanks to all concerned as I stood dazed. What in the world did the future hold now? I didn't dare think. Robert was carried shoulder high through the crowd, and I had to fight to stay with him. The TV interviews were quickly over and, shoulder high again, he was out in the street.

"I made fortune on you today, Sir," a man yelled over the crowd. "I'm only sorry I didn't get my money on when you were a 100-1 instead of just 30-1!"

Saturday's papers all carried photos and detailed accounts of the previous day's amazing events. The UUUC had captured eleven of the twelve seats. But it was one particular photo in the Belfast Telegraph that caught my eye. There was a smudge on the picture just like a bullet hole on Robert's forehead. I commented on it and was reassured it was just a smudge of ink on that one copy. I picked up other copies to check and, sure enough, it was there in every single edition. An ominous shiver went down my spine and I couldn't shake it off.

The victory parade around South Belfast was great fun and brought a real sense of relief of tension with posters Raymond had printed strung to the cars with "NICE ONE, ROBERT," his photo in the centre and the number of votes underneath.

Our people in Suffolk had been totally with us in this election as Robert had gone to great lengths to explain his thinking to them.

Leaders were organised to undertake visiting parishioners to ease Robert's work load and they seemed happy to undertake this task.

The airport was only half an hour from Suffolk, but Robert couldn't get used to the fact that, although it was only an hour's plane trip to London, it was at least three and a half hours to Westminster, and then only if all connections lined up. Then there were hold ups of fog, ice or snow and plane delays for mechanical reasons.

The Palace of Westminster, where the House of Commons and the House of Lords sit, is a world of its own. Its pomp and ceremony greet you as you come in through any of the entrances. Even the policemen are more sedate and there is a general sense of awe. I couldn't wait to see it all for myself. The day arrived and Robert phoned to see if I was all set.

"I just have to bank your pay cheque, then I'll be on my way."

"Don't bank it. Cash it and bring it with you. What the bank manager doesn't see won't worry him! We will be able to go to a show and have a meal or two out."

Our bank balance was still in technicolour, though hopefully not for too much longer.

It was going to be so special to be there for Robert's maiden speech in the House of Commons. I visualised packed seats with everyone paying rapt attention to Robert's every word. Instead, there were a total of about thirty members lazing half asleep against the amplifiers embedded in the studded green leather, oak panelled pews. It is an unwritten rule in Westminster that you don't pick holes in maiden speeches. It was not to be the case for Robert. He was thrown in at the deep end.

Robert began:
  "I believe that it is customary for an honourable member making a maiden speech to indulge in some pleasantries, but such is the grave situation in Northern Ireland that I shall have to set such pleasantries aside and get down to facts ..."

He went on to talk about South Belfast and asked:
  "When will this Honourable House give the British army—our army—and the Royal Ulster Constabulary the freedom which they need to deal effectively with terrorism? The second question which our folk are asking is when the British Government will cease deliberately missing the point. It is not enough to align the UDA and the UVF with the IRA. It is not enough to state that the Protestant extremists are as bad as Republican extremists. We deplore any man who bombs, kills or shoots in our name. He does not fight our battle. But we must remember that the violence and terrorism began with the IRA. It continues with the clear auspices of that movement and because of the ineptitude of this House and the forces under strict political control, there has been a reaction.

"For example, there was a refusal to accept power sharing in this House but, for the Ulster[4] people, it is regarded as being the only answer. The great lion of Judah has brought forth a subtle slimy snake called Sunningdale, and we are asked to accept this as British Democracy. I think that the root cause of the confusion is the fact that in Northern Ireland there is an attempt by aspirants and supporters of our sovereign state to disinherit another sovereign state. The Honourable House would never conceive of a time when, if there were enough of them, Pakistanis here would declare that this island, because they are a majority, should become a colony of Pakistan. Ulster is British. Ulster wishes to remain British. Ulster does not want to be disinherited and will not be disinherited. I had hoped that the Labour Government would indulge in honest, open government.

They made that claim. They have promised the county, and rightly so, to look again at EEC membership into which we were dragged without the consultation which had been promised. They have said that they will look for the mind of the United Kingdom on that issue. Why, then, are the Government denying the Ulster people the same right to express their opinion on a matter which is very dear to our hearts, our continued membership of this wonderful historic nation?

"We ask for nothing more than to be permitted to remain British and to have the status safeguarded, not by devious documents called the Constitution Act, but in clear, explicit terms which can and must and, I trust, will go from this Honourable House. There are faithful sons and daughters in Ulster tonight who will be waiting for the return of a prodigal mother."

Robert sat down. Mr Duffy, the member for Sheffield, Attercliffe stood up.

---

4 Loyalist Protestants tend to refer to their six counties as "Ulster" rather than "Northern Ireland" in order to emphasise their separateness from the rest of Ireland. Otherwise "Ulster" is a province of Ireland incorporating six counties of Northern Ireland and the three most northern counties of Republic of Ireland.

"The honourable member for Belfast South disclaimed at the outset of his Maiden Speech his intention to call in aid the courtesies and conventions of the House. I wish I could call them in aid in following him. I think that you in your charity, Mr Deputy Speaker, would at least expect me to welcome him to this Honourable House, but I hope you will accept that it would require a deranged sense of generosity, not only on my part but on the part of many other Honourable members, for me to compliment the Honourable member on his speech."

The scene was set. Robert was aware of the battle he was engaged in and plunged in with all his energy.

The Labour Government had the slimmest majority and, therefore, the weight of the eleven Northern Ireland members was sought on many issues. The UUUC team worked closely on this and developed strategies. Sometimes a better point was made by abstaining than by voting. But even to abstain, you had to be counted as present in the house to be counted as abstaining.

Back home, several letters appeared in the press objecting to Robert wearing his clerical collar during the election. For the first time, I was tempted to answer those complaints myself. The truth of the matter was that Robert possessed only two non-clerical shirts and ties and when these were in the wash, he had no option but to wear his clerical collar. He replied to the various criticisms stating that regarding his congregation, he had decided to ask to enter the "Secular Ministry" when his term at Suffolk was completed. "The Secular Ministry," Robert explained, "simply means ... that one expresses His spiritual and moral awareness in the wider community without having pastoral responsibility for a particular congregation." He said that he intended to reside in the community and continue preaching the gospel in whatever opportunities presented themselves. Another important consideration was that as a Christian Minister in Parliament, he could help formulate and implement "moral" legislation and in doing so achieve something normally beyond the reach of a parish minister. He argued that prevention is better than cure and that if we had more Christians in Parliament, we might have less questionable legislation.

The terrorists with their twisted minds went into full swing with a campaign of enticing policemen into traps, and so began a new phase of the war. Two policemen were gunned down in Dunmurry near our manse.

"The killing of two loyal servants of the community is too infuriating for words," Robert said. "All decent men will demand the ruthless pursuit of the murderers until they are brought to justice. How many more deaths must occur before Westminster stops playing politics with Ulster's blood?"

In April, a serious situation had developed, and Ulster found itself in the middle of a Loyalist Protestant Workers' Strike that literally closed Northern Ireland. Many politicians tried to negotiate to get the workers back to work, feeling the time was not right for such a drastic move, but Ulster had had enough. Robert appealed to the press:
"There is still real hope of political progress."

Merlyn Rees, the secretary of State for Northern Ireland, was reported as sticking to his attitude of refusing to negotiate with the strikers.

It was reported by the Northern Ireland Office that the strikers had failed to turn up for the meeting. Whatever the truth was, there was a complete stalemate, at least until Harold Wilson made his now infamous speech, referring to the people of Ulster as "Spongers."

Ulster rose en masse in fury and the strike began in earnest, with politicians backing it. Electricity was cut off for longer and longer periods, except in areas where there was a hospital, though even hospitals were affected too at times. Food began to be in short supply as shops joined in. Petrol and other vital supplies couldn't get through the roadblocks that were set up and manned by Loyalist workers.

Overall, these roadblocks remained peaceful unless someone they did not regard as an essential worker tried to get through. Nurses, doctors and other essential workers had to produce identification to pass through. Farmers were hardest hit financially as they lost whole batches of chickens and other livestock without electricity and heating.

In hospitals, life was very difficult. Despite having backup generators, many operating theatres could not function. Musgrave Park Hospital where I worked was one such case. If the electricity went off during an operation, the changeover to a generator would have caused a cloud of dust, which meant we could only do emergency work. The blessing of the idle time was in-depth conversations about the Lord with colleagues who were really searching for truth.

After a long day spent knitting and waiting for emergency work, I arrived home to find Robert in the dining room trying to cook a meal for us. He had lit the fire and was sitting with a saucepan on it heating up some processed peas. Beside him he had another tin of stewed meat and another of new potatoes, all from our back-up larder. The whole scene looked so unappetising that my hunger left me. I managed to persuade him to put them all together in one large saucepan. At least they would all be hot together. Towser and Boo ate well that night! Opponents of the strike also had a hard time, as they were prevented from getting to work. We found that battery radio was the surest form of communication as the electricity interruptions, meant that we couldn't depend on the television.

In the estates around South Belfast, as in many parts of Ulster, a system was worked out to ensure that no elderly person suffered. Milk and coal were distributed to them. Camping apparatus was hauled out of attics and caravans and put to use in many homes.

The Ulster Workers Council was calling for early Assembly elections and the scrapping of the Sunningdale agreement. We had thought they would have been automatic after the Westminster elections in February and the massive Ulster 421,782 anti-Sunningdale vote to 295,858 pro-Sunningdale vote. Finally, the Executive at Stormont fell, and the strike ended with rejoicing and celebration. Hillsborough farmers headed one celebration cavalcade with a trailer containing three donkeys called Gerry, Paddy and Brian, supposedly representing the leaders of the defeated coalition parties.

The Methodist Church Conference in June was to be held in Cork. Knowing it was going to be a rough ride for Robert, I arranged some time off and went along. As we had to travel through the Republic of Ireland to get to the Conference, arrangements had been made to give us a Garda escort. At that stage we were unaware that the terrorists had Garda sympathisers and some even more than sympathisers. As we travelled down the island of Ireland, our Garda escort changed.

By our third or fourth change, we were already very late but resigned that we couldn't change the situation. Our latest Garda companions flagged us down.

"You're rather late, Sir," he said, saluting as Robert wound the window down.

"Yes, I'm afraid so." Robert tried not to sound impatient.

"We are going to hit a lot of traffic from here on. Keep right on our tail and we'll see if we can get you through."

With that, we started up again with them in front now, headlights full on and sirens blazing. We proceeded up the centre of the road. The traffic parted like the waves of the Red Sea so we stuck to them like glue and in no time at all we went through what would have been a real bottleneck but it was fun.

Arriving in Cork City, I dropped Robert at Wesley Chapel and proceeded to the boarding house that the Conference had allocated for us. The slight, middle-aged woman who opened the door to me, proceeded me up the narrow hall past her Holy Water font to her dining room, wringing her hands.

"There's a mistake." Her eyes were frightened. I told them "I couldn't have Garda watching the house—bad for business, you know. You do understand?"

She was miserably shifting from foot to foot, wringing her hands in her anxiety to persuade me to go.

"They should have told you. Not to let you come here."

I tried to explain that I hadn't called by the Conference, but she wasn't listening, so I picked up the suitcases and made for the door. She was obviously terrified that her house would be a target for the IRA, and I felt sorry for her. We were relocated by the Conference to a city centre hotel.

As the week went on, Robert became more and more alienated from his colleagues. They didn't seem to want to know about the "Methodists Awake" campaign despite the 8,000 signatures of support.

I sat in on some sessions, but at other times when the topic was not relevant to me, I shopped or went sunbathing at a local beach. The Garda stayed on duty at Wesley Chapel while Robert was inside. I got irritated at finding them constantly asleep. (They didn't care.) So when I picked Robert up one evening for a trip out west, I decided I would shake them up. I took off through the traffic like a rocket, without even waiting to see if they had noticed our departure. It was rush hour. I wove in and out of traffic and gave them a terrible time.

Once out of town, I had to ease up as there was no traffic. The friends we planned to visit lived right out in the countryside down a maze of country lanes. These lanes were totally devoid of signposts and, unless you knew your way, you got lost. I knew my way well and sped around each corner, navigated Y junctions, crossroads, avoiding potholes and bad curves. When we reached the farm, our escort climbed out of their car rather slowly and asked Robert rather sheepishly if he could direct them back to Clonakilty town. They laughed together as Robert gave them directions.

He then released a statement:-
"I am a Methodist and will always remain a Methodist Minister. I intend to go to the United States later this year, with a view to becoming associated with a Methodist Conference which would enable me to continue preaching Methodism in Ulster."

We had discovered, to our dismay, that Robert's ordination as a Methodist Minister could be removed if he did not hold a weekly meeting and, that being his only qualification, we were fearful for our future. Another election was looming on the horizon, and we wondered whether he would fall between two stools.

"We can always emigrate," he would tease.

At that point I would have gladly moved anywhere else, but I knew we were in Northern Ireland for a reason, and we had to learn to lean on God. Our congregation was still with us, and they lavished love and support on us.

My family, and particularly my Mum, were having a tough time with it all. She had been a Methodist her whole life, and there had never been anyone in our connection involved in politics. Someone kindly said to her one day out of the blue, "You must be so proud of your son-in-law."

She shared what she'd been feeling, we reconciled, and the distance between us disappeared. It had hurt so much to be separated from my family, yet we knew we were in God's will and timing!

As we began to think seriously about setting up our own home elsewhere, I awoke in a sweat one night and counted up our main possessions. They consisted of two rocking chairs, a twin-tub washing machine, a small fridge, a double bed and a hearth rug. Now don't get me wrong, many people have much less, though not usually after four years of married life. It was not much to set up a new home with, so Robert approached the Housing Executive about renting a flat, knowing the only place we could get accommodation quickly, was in Suffolk. We had to be out of the manse in a few week's time in order to allow our replacement to move in, so we went on to the Emergency Housing List. No one wanted to live in Suffolk, so our chances were good.

Robert meanwhile, headed off to America with a vague address to contact some Methodist churches in the southern States of Mississippi, Alabama and Louisiana.

When he landed in Jackson, Mississippi, Robert was met by Rev. Ben Gerald, the then president of the Mississippi Conference of the Methodist Protestant Church. Ben took Robert to his home and then to some churches he wanted to visit. Nothing was too much trouble for Ben and yet he put absolutely no pressure on Robert.

Robert found there was an affinity between himself and Ben's people and decided that, provided they would have him, he would like to join them officially. A celebration meal was organised, and several dignitaries and ministers were invited. They were all seated around a large table chatting and enjoying their newfound friendship while the waitress worked her way around the table taking each person's order. She came to Robert and with a straight face he ordered his meal and a double brandy. A stunned silence ensued. Robert pretended not to notice and continued chatting until his laughter erupted at the sight of all their shocked faces.

"Cancel that order," Robert called to the waitress. She couldn't have served him anyhow as it was a teetotal hotel. How Robert enjoyed this joke at the expense of his new teetotal colleagues!

Back home, the Housing Executive notified me of two vacant two-bedroom flats, and rather apprehensively, I collected the keys and went to see them. The first was in a high-rise block which wouldn't have been suitable for dogs. It was also the same block where a young woman had committed suicide. Robert and the police had to break in. She had been having it rough for quite some time and had stayed in our home. I didn't imagine that Robert would have slept easy there.

The next was a first floor flat on a corner, with just one flat below it. The main problem was that it looked directly into the Catholic Ladybrook estate, and the chance of a sniper attack was very real. I asked the police for advice and they felt, as I did, that anywhere in Suffolk was dangerous and we were taking a chance. But if we took it, they promised to make the doors and windows bullet proof as soon as possible, so I told the Housing Executive that I would take it.

I consoled myself that we would only be there for six months and during that time we would have saved enough money for a deposit on a house of our own. The rise in salary from £1,000 per annum as a minister to an MP's pay of £4,500 seemed enormous to me, and I was sure we would soon be able to buy our own home, not appreciating how expensive life in London would be for overnight stays and meals. Robert arrived back home from the USA jubilant about his newfound Methodist friends. He felt that they were "true-blue" Methodists, evangelical in outlook and very nice people as well. God had prospered their church through adversity.

I was trying to be as excited as possible about the flat, but he was not terribly thrilled with the location of it and reluctantly agreed to help with the painting, at least until he was called away on sudden urgent business! Our new home was beginning to take shape, and I was delighted to think we owned all the furnishings. In the manse we had constantly had to take care to replace anything we damaged or broke. This was all ours!

The Suffolk congregation arranged a farewell evening for us. It was a great evening with musical items secretly rehearsed by the choir and soloists. Each organisation presented us with gifts—a gold watch from the choir, a lamp from the Girl's Brigade, a luxury duvet and so on. Robert was presented with a cheque for £100 and a special scout award called a "Thanks" badge. It became a treasured possession which he wore proudly. Rev. Day Ludlow gave an address, but I don't remember much of it as I was fighting back tears.

As Robert closed with the last words, I wiped my eyes and became conscious of Robert's voice as he finished: "Don't remember Robert. Remember rather Robert Bradford's Saviour."

He sat down beside me, very pale. I knew he was finding it as hard as I was, even harder. Robert ended the service with a benediction.

"And now may the grace of the Lord Jesus Christ, the love of God and the friendship of the Holy Spirit be with you all, until Christ comes or calls."

As he did, my mind wandered back to the times we'd had together.

Incredible blessing had been poured out on us in Suffolk—new believers added to the Kingdom, true friendship and wonderful times of fellowship and praise. I thought of the young people whom we had managed to pull away from the influences of alcohol, drugs, terrorism, and even the occult. The house was brimming with youth on Sunday nights, bodies were in every room, on the stairs playing guitar and in the bathroom. You threw them out when it was needed, but the leaded glass front door panel that was left bulging outwards every week, I had to carefully ease back into shape with fear and trembling.

I thought of the Women's Department when time and again speakers, who had been booked, phoned to say they couldn't or wouldn't come because of danger. How those long-suffering ladies were treated time and again to our holiday slides, me attempting to lead choruses with a guitar, a quickly organised bible quiz, or whatever I could come up with at short notice.

We walked out of that beautiful building with very heavy hearts. We knew that although we would be living just around the corner in the flat, we would not be able to attend services. The Methodists' unwritten rule that you don't go back to your previous congregation for a year to allow a new minister to settle in, definitely applied to us. Anyone might find it difficult to follow Robert in normal circumstances because he always threw himself one hundred percent into anything he did and because of the sheer volume of work he got through. The fact that he was practically regarded as a saint in the area would make it a difficult task and one that we were not about to make even more difficult. It was only a matter of days before we moved to the flat in the back of a van borrowed from a local shopkeeper. There we would have to shut our door on all the problems around us and stay aloof, a very difficult task when we cared so much.

A new era was about to begin for us and not a very pleasant one.

Chapter 8

The Queen, America and Home Security

The flat was terribly noisy. We had no carpets for the first while, so every sound seemed to echo and the dogs, unused to the constant traffic, were barking continually. I had visions of the Housing Executive evicting us. I felt sorry for the neighbours who had to put up with us. The worst came at night. With our flat being on a corner and the garden having been allowed to grow wild, every dog in the neighbourhood seemed to congregate there for turf warfare.

We barely had our feet on the ground when another election was called. There had been so much negative publicity about our departure from the church that we wondered how the public would react when it came to voting. I had made a point of buying two new suits, new shirts and ties for Robert, as his black clerical suits now seemed so out of place.

At least we won't have people complaining about his clerical collar, I thought.

The election was fought with a different emphasis this time. Robert summed it up for the press like this:

> *"The Constitution must be secured with full parity with the rest of the United Kingdom assured. Second, the basic right of United Kingdom citizenship must be safeguarded by a determined security policy which will isolate and root out the terrorists. Third, the*

industrial and social problems must be tackled forcibly, especially the chronic housing shortage, to which I have given much of my time. Fourth, a realistic and lasting peace must be sought, enabling every law-abiding citizen, irrespective of religion, to enjoy our province."

A big boost came to the UUUC when the Right Honourable Enoch Powell joined the ranks to fight for the cause and stand for election in South Down. Polling day was Thursday 10th October 1974. By the time the polls were closed, we were confident of victory and also relieved that at least for the next while, Robert had a job.

The South Belfast count was generally the first to be called with West Belfast close on its heels. With an electorate of 75,443, Robert had gained an increase of 30,116 votes. He took the opportunity to blast the press for what he felt was their unfair treatment of him. That was a big mistake. Politicians depend heavily on the press, because if they are not quoted in the papers or seen on TV or heard on the radio, the general public assumes they are not working, and so the press joined ranks by ignoring him.

The Westminster soccer team selected Robert to play for them. He was thrilled because he was finding the change of physical pace since becoming an MP very difficult. He was now gaining weight.

Further adjustments were necessary on Sundays. Instead of preaching, we were free to attend different churches. This was a great pleasure, as we had rarely been able to sit in church together since we were married. However, we could not find a particular church that we wanted to commit to. He liked the solid Presbyterian teaching, but I disliked their music style. Great Victoria Street Baptist suited us better, but we didn't settle yet.

Preaching appointments became scarce and Robert had to face the humiliation of ministers refusing to have him in their pulpits. They assumed that because he was a politician, he couldn't preach the gospel, and he was deeply hurt by this. He regarded the pulpit as sacred, reserved for preaching the gospel. Never in all his time at Suffolk had he mentioned politics from the pulpit. In fact, the opposite was true. Whenever he was invited to speak at a political rally, he would always include preaching the gospel. He regarded South Belfast as his parish and his 75,000 constituents as parishioners, and treated them as such, regardless of their political persuasion, taking endless time in his advice centres to listen to people's problems and concerns.

He felt the urgency of our Lord's near return and didn't want to miss a single opportunity to share the gospel, so we began fasting one day a week, a habit we kept up for many years. An invite arrived for him to speak at a conference at Corrymeela, Ballycastle. The conference speakers included politicians of all persuasions and included some Republic of Ireland government officials. When we arrived, the only politician in sight was Peter McLachlan. The debate got under way with the theme, "Ulster politics and Christian morality." Robert spoke:

> *"The problems of Northern Ireland are the result of three things: the Roman Catholic Church, International Marxism and ecumenical confusion. I believe that Scripture can be interpreted and understood very clearly in the light of current events."*

He elaborated and went on to say:

> *"If the UK is to survive, the violent elements whose purpose it is to destroy must be dealt with and if that involves killing, then that has got to be."*

The debate began in earnest with 30 or so people attacking Robert from all sides. There was a pause and a man sitting opposite spoke:

> *"I think we are doing Mr. Bradford an injustice."*
> *At last, one level–headed person is present,* I thought. I relaxed a little.

*"We are treating him as a rational, sane person, when he is obviously
nothing of the sort."*

And so it continued hot and heavy, with Robert responding to all
they threw at him. He tried to lighten the atmosphere.

*"I'm beginning to feel like a mangy old lion being thrown to the
Christians."*

There was some laughter, but it didn't achieve the desired effect. The
house was divided.

No matter how hard we tried, we did not succeed in buying a house.

Then came the bright idea of buying a plot of land and building on
it, with the thought this might be cheaper, but plots were in short
supply. We discovered that a friend owned some land in New Forge
Lane in South Belfast, and we purchased it.

Robert eased any concerns I had by telling me, "Even if we can't keep
up the payments, we can always sell it at a profit."

The salary that had seemed so enormous to us at the start was obviously
not meant to be a sole source of income. Most of the other MPs had
jobs, but as Robert rarely took payment for preaching, my salary was
really needed. Robert would take constituents out for coffee or for
a meal in London at our expense. I urged him to cut back, but his
attitude was that this was an experience of a lifetime for each one and
was not to be denied them.

I was at work in theatre one day when I looked up to see Sister
Connolly looking intently at me. My heart missed a beat. I knew
instantly there was something wrong with Robert. My mind was
questioning if he had been shot.

She assured me it was not a shooting but that he had taken ill on the flight home from London. He had been taken to the City Hospital with severe pain in one leg. I immediately thought of deep venous thrombosis. She assured me that it might not be as Robert was still conscious. Another nurse was already scrubbing up to take over from me. My mask was soggy with tears, and I couldn't see to hand the instruments to the surgeon. I tried to cope by looking sideways, knowing I would contaminate the whole tray if my tears fell on it or if I breathed through a sodden mask onto an open wound. It seemed an age before the other nurse took over.

I don't remember the short drive to the City Hospital, just the look on Robert's ashen face in Casualty. He was lying on a trolley looking very ill indeed. His colleague John Carson, the MP from North Belfast, was with him.

"He wanted to go home, but I insisted he came here," John told me.

I was so grateful as Robert's blood pressure was barely readable. What were the possibilities if this clot broke up? A heart attack? A stroke? Finally, he was transferred to a medical ward under a Dr. Connon.

The doctor had already gone off duty so the ward sister explained that a lung scan had revealed that Robert had multiple emboli and told me that the next 24 hours would be crucial. The heparinised drip was in place and I sat down beside Robert again and tried to lift his spirits for the remainder of visiting time. By now he was alert enough to chat and told me what had happened. He had woken in his rather crummy bed-sit, close to Westminster, to find he had a severe leg cramp. He was keen to catch the early flight back to Belfast and had bashed his leg around to relieve the spasm. Now I understood why he had multiple emboli! Despite the fact the spasm did not lift, he had hobbled on to the plane, but started to feel ill shortly after lift-off. He tried to tap the shoulder of a passenger in front of him but was too weak. He had thought he was dying and prayed telling God he was already 30,000 feet up and perhaps the Lord could just take him on up to Heaven and end this horrendous pain.

He came to just as the plane landed and was whisked off to the City Hospital despite his protests. I didn't dare tell him that if he had gone home to bed, he would probably have died. I had a dreadful night waiting to hear news of Robert and phoned work to say I wouldn't be in until later. I went straight to his ward and found him waiting for a gastroscopy. I felt sorry for him as I often had to assist them and knew it would not be a pleasant experience for him. He was quite cheerful.

I got a chance to talk to Dr. Connon who told me, "I think he's almost out of danger now." He suspected that the severe flu Robert had a couple of weeks previously might have caused a roughening of the vein in his leg, allowing a clot to develop. He assured me that if his diagnosis was correct, Robert would have no further trouble, but that he was authorising a gastroscopy to make sure anticoagulants weren't going to bleed from Robert's old ulcer site. After that he would be prescribed warfarin and sent home.

Robert wasn't an easy patient, and I felt sorry for the nurses. Late one evening I was about to leave the ward when the night Superintendent came in. She started to fuss that the high window above his head was open. Robert leapt up, heparin drip attached, stood on his pillows and pushed it closed. I thought the poor woman was going to have a stroke!

He told me that he'd had a visit from the hospital chaplain who had told him how dangerous a clot could be, but I was furious to hear about this "Job's comforter."

I was due some holiday leave, so off to Dublin we went for a few days.

Normally, we were meant to inform our local police if we ventured into the Republic of Ireland. They would then have to inform the

Garda, and, in turn, that information could be leaked. Many times the terrorists fled over the border after a murder and somehow didn't get caught by the Garda or the Republic's army, and that kept happening for 30 years. Because of that uncertainty, we didn't inform anyone, feeling we would be safer if no one knew.

As soon as we arrived home, Parliament made the decision to stay in the Common Market. Robert was infuriated with the decision and went into an Anglican Church to meditate and read the page in the prayer book for that day:

"Therefore hear the Word of the Lord, you scoffers who rule this people in Jerusalem. Because you have said, 'We have made a covenant with death, and with Sheol we have an agreement; when the overflowing scourge passes through, it will not come to us, for we have made lies our refuge, and in falsehood we have taken shelter.' Therefore thus says the Lord God: 'Behold I lay in Zion a foundation stone, a tested stone, a precious cornerstone, of a sure foundation; He who believes will not be in haste and I will make justice the line and righteousness the plummet; and the hail will sweep away the refuge of lies, and the waters will overflow the shelter. Then your covenant with death will be annulled, and your agreement with Sheol will not stand; when the overflowing scourge passes through, you will be beaten down by it, as often as it passes it will take you, for morning by morning it will pass through, and by day and night; it will be sheer terror to understand the message. For the bed is too short to stretch oneself on it, and the covering too narrow to wrap oneself in it'" (Isaiah 28:14 – 20, RSV).

Very soon, we were back to a normal routine, so every night Robert would phone when in London to talk over the day's events. Bill Craig and he often escaped from Westminster to go and have a meal together when the pressure of those endless speeches became too much. I was grateful to Bill as he was expanding Robert's culinary tastes, which encouraged me as I enjoyed cooking.

America, here we come...

In nursing, I received many days off a year for holidays, so I saved them all up and then planned a four-week trip to Mississippi in order for Robert to take four separate week-long missions. He had told me so much about these lovely people he had met, and I couldn't wait to meet them also.

Rev. Ben Gerald met us at the airport in Jackson, Mississippi in the early hours of the morning and took us to his house. They were a gentle, quiet family who made us feel at home.

The next morning, I experienced jetlag for the first time. Robert was preaching and within five minutes of him standing up, he went from one Robert to three Roberts. How Robert managed to preach, I've no idea. To this day, I don't know what was said in that meeting as all my strength was spent in trying to remain focused.

Ben took us to "Dinner on the ground" at the Vicksburg church where we were to spend our first week's mission or "Revival" as the Americans called it. Each family had brought a dish of food, and the church hall was packed with the congregation eating from paper plates on their knees. The food was different from what I was used to and I tried a little of everything. Their habit of mixing sweet and savoury salads together was a new experience—I loved it. A gospel group that had played at the morning service stayed and played throughout the afternoon. It was a delight to get to know these American Christians, then go into the church, spend some time listening to the gospel in song, then wander out and chat to more people. The whole day was given to fellowshipping at the church, and everyone enjoyed it so much.

"This is how it should be," I thought. "Being a Christian should be joyful. If only the folks back home could capture this joy, life would be so much easier."

The evening service was a happy time for all with contributions from the group and the choir, and I had my first taste of their praise services. A chorus leader conducted the piano and organ as well as the congregational singing. The result was overwhelming.

Robert preached better than I had ever heard him and despite his accent, people seemed to have no problem understanding him. The congregation paid for time on their local radio to broadcast their services, thus evangelising to their area.

"Let me introduce you both to Mr. and Mrs. Bruce."

It was their minister, Brand Jenkins, introducing us to the people we were to stay with. Webb was tall and thin with an all-American crew cut, while Florence had a lovely, warm smile. We became close friends. They visited us in Northern Ireland, and we tried to visit anytime we came to America.

Our cases were transferred to the Bruce's beautiful Oldsmobile and we were whisked off to their home. As we drove slowly down the gravel driveway, we saw a rustic, brick bungalow set amongst high trees, a really peaceful setting. Behind the bungalow, the land sloped down to a lake. A crazy paving path and steps led through the towering trees to a small private jetty. It was a small piece of Heaven on Earth, and I was thinking, *How will I keep Robert in line for a whole week for these quiet, retired folks?*

We weren't in the house two minutes before Robert had his shoes off and his feet on the hearth.

"Will you behave?" I whispered in a strong tone.

He replied, "We have to stay here for a week. They won't mind!"

He grinned mischievously.

Thank goodness he doesn't have smelly feet, I thought.

Our second mission was in West Monroe, Louisiana. It was a totally different experience. Robert had met Rev. Johnny Hankin, the young minister, on a previous visit, and he came to drive us to Louisiana on the Friday night after the service. He explained that he had wanted us to stay with them in their trailer, but a couple who always put up visiting speakers had been offended at the suggestion.

"They are very difficult to wake," Johnny said hesitantly as we stood ringing the doorbell after our long journey into the early hours of the morning.

Fifteen minutes later when we had created a racket fit to waken the dead, a sleepy woman's head, bedecked in curlers, peered around the door. Johnny had warned us that she never stopped talking and within twenty minutes, we knew what he meant. She hadn't stopped to draw a breath. Her husband didn't appear until breakfast time. Very tired and overfed, we would happily have skipped breakfast but couldn't risk offending our hosts.

The week in Monroe, Louisiana was totally different again. The church was equally beautiful but in a different way. The people in both places were so hospitable that it proved to be a problem for us. We were given a hearty breakfast of American biscuits or scones, scrambled eggs, bacon and coffee and then we would be in someone else's house for lunch and somewhere else for an evening meal, followed by supper after church. By the end of the second week, we both felt ill. It was hard to turn down such lavish hospitality. As in Vicksburg, each housewife only had one chance to entertain us and so each produced mountainous quantities of lovely food. Thank goodness Johnny and Bonnie Hankins understood, having been on Revival themselves, and helped us cut out some meals without causing offense.

One man took some photos of us and at the end of the week his wife presented us with some sketches she had done of us. She liked to use her God-given talent to the glory of God after being healed of a serious illness.

The third week was to be spent in Monticello, a small country town, staying in a motel. A very different time was organised by the minister Rev. Dr. Sellers, with Robert speaking to students in the local university in the mornings, and fewer scheduled meal sessions.

It was a small community centred on a crossroads, and people were easy to get to know.

A tragic story emerged out of that small community. A young couple had lost both of their children in a fire at their home but what should have been two miserable people turned out to be two shining rays of sunshine for the Lord. Their testimony of how the Lord had helped them and brought them through their tragedy was awe inspiring.

Their attitude was that God had allowed them to have two precious children for a short time, and they were grateful as others had never experienced that.

Our last week was to be spent in Alabama in a little town called Thomasville. We were informed that it was "out in the sticks," and this was not a joke as we discovered when we traversed the dirt roads.

On our way down, Dr. Sellers hinted, "They get up rather early down here, and they're inclined to expect you to do the same."

Hopefully they won't tonight, I thought, as it was already Saturday, and we didn't expect to get there until the small hours of the morning.

The manse turned out to be a wooden bungalow and the Pastors greeted us and showed us straight to our room.

Those pretty net curtains aren't going to keep out much of the early morning sun, I thought.

Despite something howling in the forest beside us, we fell asleep quickly with exhaustion. A few minutes later, well that's what it felt like, the door practically fell off its hinges with the hammering of a fist.

"Breakfast!" someone yelled.

We thought for a moment that we were back in Belfast as Robert sat bolt upright in bed and opened his mouth to reply, none too politely, so I stuffed a pillow on his face and shut him up. I released him when our host's footsteps had faded away.

"They can't be serious, what time is it?" he said exasperated.

We looked at our watches. It was 5.45 a.m. and the sun was still trying to get out of its bed. We'd only arrived a few hours earlier. I quickly pulled on some clothes, assuring him I would go and that he should have a lie in. Before I got our door closed behind me, Robert was out cold.

Robert preached that week and on the last night the whole congregation lined up to shake our hands and some even had tears in their eyes.

All the tests were done, yet pregnancy hadn't ensued. It was a very difficult time for us as a couple. Folks would even ask, "Aren't you thinking of having a family soon?" They couldn't know how excruciating those comments were to my battered soul. In extreme circumstances I'd even reply, "Nope. I'm a career woman," just to get them to stop. It was breaking my heart.

We arrived home to face the prospect of yet another childless Christmas only to find that God had planned a glorious surprise—a little girl of

18 months for us to adopt. The unspeakable joy that that gave us is impossible to describe. We had great fun buying nursery furniture and clothes in anticipation of her arrival. As all new parents know, that first Christmas would be a magical time for us. This precious daughter was everything we had hoped and prayed for.

Grandad Jimmy had painted the spare flat room in advance, not understanding why I wanted the ceiling pink!

"No one paints ceilings pink," he protested, "they're always white!"

"Yes," I said, "but I want her to feel warm and cosy in this new home.

In her cot she'll be gazing at the ceiling a lot, there's actually no law that says we have to!"

He relented, and the grimy motorbike workshop that the previous tenants had made the room into was transformed as new wallpaper, curtains and carpet were added.

Our lives would now revolve around this precious new family member. But all was not going to be easy. Getting her to sleep was an impossible task because she didn't yet trust us but, understandably, had to have us in sight. This meant long hours cramped on the floor of her room with her determination to watch with at least one eye open. When you thought she had fallen asleep and were about to exit the room thinking, she would bounce up and we were back to square one.

My Mum, super keen to meet and hug her newest grandchild came often, and she gave me great advice in the sleep routine.

Robert was back in Parliament again so I was left to get on with things. From working full time and being out every evening at church meetings, I found I had little to occupy me despite the extra laundry and learning to be a parent. When we ventured out with the pram and dogs on leads, all the local pooches would appear which was a nightmare. It became scarier until Boo refused to even venture out to the back area and began to relieve herself in the flat, much to my horror.

This confined life of the flat was becoming extremely difficult. Robert was constantly under pressure in London, then had advice centres to attend on Saturdays and Mondays. And with the police advising him he shouldn't have a set routine, Robert's concern was for the pensioners. He did not want them going out of their way or having to pay extra bus fares to get to see him.

Robert had kept very quiet on the subject of garden parties at Buckingham Palace, and it was a while before I discovered we could put our names in a hat in the hope of being picked to go. When I mentioned this, his face looked tragic as pound signs began spinning before his eyes while he thought of me shopping for an outfit. Add to that the fact that he hated to dress up for anything, even weddings (we were always the last to arrive and the first to leave, sometimes before the bride and groom). I was unsure if the Garden Party was going to be a party or a demise with the pressure.

In 1977 an invitation arrived:
The Lord Chamberlain is
Commanded by Her Majesty to invite
The Reverent Robert Bradford and Mrs. Bradford to an
Afternoon Party in the Garden of Buckingham Palace.

We set off for the airport and you know when you know that something is missing? I looked at Robert and he was there—check! Suitcases were there—check! I was there—check! Then it occurred to me that the invitation was still on the mantelpiece and so was our pass to the palace. Without those we would not get in. We had to turn round, go back and catch the next Aircraft shuttle flight. Then it was a mad rush to get ready in the Family Room of the House of Commons with others also trying to get dressed.

Finally, we arrived at the appropriate gate, and I was dragged up a long, gravel path at a brisk pace. I was out of breath as I was whisked past the beautiful lake with its stately pink flamingos onto the lawn where people were lining up in three groups preparing to meet their royal hosts.

"I've arranged for us to be introduced to the Queen," Robert said over his shoulder as he charged on with determination to get through the crowds.

I gulped and held on to his hand tightly saying "Excuse me, excuse me" as we pushed into the centre. The man in charge of introductions spotted Robert and pulled us through the lines to a position where we would be introduced.

As Her Majesty, Queen Elizabeth, approached, talking graciously to those she met, she would walk first to one side and then to the other to speak to people who weren't being formally introduced, knowing it was the experience of a lifetime for so many.

The closer the Queen came to me, my knees were knocking, legs shaking like Elvis. My mind started to go blank: How do I address her? Ma'am? What on earth will she ask me? How should I answer, or am I not allowed to? Suddenly, she was standing in front of us smiling. I managed a wobbly curtsey, hoping I wouldn't fall in my stilettos.

Knowing she must speak first, the Queen began to chat. I don't remember what she said. Robert did most of the replying. Waiting for an opportune time, he said, "Your loyal people in Ulster are looking forward so much to your impending Jubilee visit to your Province and pray that you will come and go in safety."

She took her leave of us. I thought with relief that I had survived remarkably well, that the worst was over until Robert grabbed my hand, and we took off again.

"Calm down. Surely we can relax now?" I said.

"Don't you want to meet the Duke of Edinburgh?" His eyes twinkled as he rushed on.

We pushed into another row and again we were spotted and placed in position. I survived yet another curtsey without falling over as my heels sank into the grass.

We then made our way to the tea tent and helped ourselves to buffet style goodies and a cup of tea. We sank into two vacant chairs, and I sighed with relief. We reminisced over the last chaotic half hour and the thrill of it all.

An invitation to a reception at Hillsborough Castle came through our door regarding the Queen's visit to Northern Ireland. Without doubt I told Robert, "A new outfit is definitely in order in case the Queen recognised my last one." Robert held his head with feigned despair but secretly enjoyed my excitement.

The sun was shining over Hillsborough Castle as we walked through the lawn. We entered the crowd and took our positions as her majesty walked by. Spotting Robert she came over.

"Haven't I met you before?" she smiled.

Robert bowed as the group parted for him,
"We were introduced at your garden party last month. My name is
Bradford."

"Ah yes," she said, "I remember." They chatted for a few minutes further,
but Robert couldn't get over the fact that she had remembered him.

"She must be introduced to hundreds of people every week. Imagine
her remembering my face!"

"Once seen, never forgotten," I teased.

Robert was becoming aware of how widespread pornography had
become and how it was easily available to young age groups. He
began to investigate how to prevent this access and to fight to secure
peace in our beloved province.

Any terrorism organisation works off two things: fear and money.

They create fear and they are funded by money. Knowing this, Robert
was working to get to the roots of IRA terrorist-funding operations.

He began to collect a lot of information about their fund-raising
activities and investigated possible links with the Royal Victoria
Hospital.

An interesting campaign of sending unwanted parcels to us began.

There were pink suits ordered for Robert, books, unwanted gifts,
insurance men invited to call, anything the people responsible
thought would annoy us. For the most part we found it hilarious
and couldn't wait to see what we would receive next. The annoyance
was in humping large parcels to the post office to return them. It
seemed to be mainly a one-person campaign, as we discovered from

the address which always began with "Wine Lodge." We had both been brought up to be strictly teetotal and this was hardly a name we would use for our home.

We began to think seriously about building on our plot of land, and I threw myself into planning what kind of house I would like and designing it. It was lovely to start from scratch and plan it just as we wanted. We chatted to an architect, and the design he produced had no resemblance to what I'd specified so we tried another. He understood my thinking, and we began in earnest. It was a sloping piece of land, so the design needed to incorporate that. The front was a bungalow to the road with stairs down to the bedrooms. An office space and garage were under the house with access to the back garden and a planned football pitch and vegetable patch.

The architect complimented me that he couldn't better my design.

After what seemed interminable months, the plans went out for tender, and building work began. The sloping ground meant that piling the land was necessary to secure the foundations. I was standing on the muddy ground late one evening (a hired company had just finished the piles) when, with plans in hand, I was trying to make sense of the positioning of the steel sticking out of the mud. I sauntered over to the builder, a lovely big Catholic gentleman, and asked, "Would you show me where you've positioned the piles in relation to the building?" He proceeded to point them out on the blueprint. I was horrified. I looked at him and said, "That's west!" pointing at the setting sun on the hills before us. I reached over and turned the plans in his hands by 180 degrees. He blanched! Extra piles were inserted to make up the deficit, and we got extra basement office space because of the mistake. Our new home took about twelve months to build. We borrowed a large van and with the help of my mum, my sister Mar, my brother Dermot and friends, we shifted our furniture from the flat and the various attics where we'd stored our boxes. We had two rooms completed in the house allowing us to move our stuff in. I had already made all the curtains and Wee Jimmy put up curtain rails for me so that we could have some privacy. As yet, there was no kitchen, and the builder rigged up a standpipe for me so that at least we had access to water. Dermot leant us his camping washstand. Talk about going from a palace to emptiness, except the flat was not a palace by any stretch, but the new home was definitely empty!

It was almost Christmas. The front garden still had to be built up and a path laid but for now we had a couple of walking planks across the mud and a gang plank over a four-foot drop at the front door.

It was terrifying watching the men manoeuvre the piano across the plank. The trolley it was resting on got stuck, swaying halfway, and I watched in disbelief as the men tried to steady it. It survived and although slightly out of tune, was none the worse for the move.

My brother Morley visited, and I remember welcoming him across the very wobbly plank. He was not too steady on his feet, but he manoeuvred it successfully. It was within the first few days that a neighbour came to introduce herself, bringing a housewarming present of a lovely fruitcake. I couldn't have been more thrilled to find I had lovely neighbours again. Our neighbours in Suffolk also had been really helpful. On one occasion, the fan belt had gone in our car and Wee Jimmy had come up to fix it while Robert was in London, and I was out. Several of them had walked over to tackle him to see who he was and why he was touching our car.

Getting our new house finished took a long time but we coped with all that, and all the tensions we had been suffering eased considerably. We had a big lounge with a large picture window facing east which got the morning sun and one to the back with a view of Divis Mountain, which took in some glorious sunsets and vast gardens for dogs and our daughter to let off energy in.

Robert purchased a desk and carpet tiles for his basement office and even laid the carpet tiles himself, much to the amusement of Wee Jimmy, who knew that Robert's record with practical work was zero.

His enthusiasm did not stretch to decorating the rest of the house. Our kitchen was fitted on Christmas Eve.

We had a lot of entertaining to do to make up for the three years in the flat. Sundays were now fairly hectic with Robert having lots of preaching engagements. It had taken all this time to build up to services every Sunday, but now he was really in demand again, and he loved it. He felt that it was a huge release to preach which allowed him to cope with the strain of Westminster.

Mondays and Tuesdays I fed my freezer for the next weekend's entertaining. Wednesdays and Thursdays, I worked night duty in the Ulster Hospital Cardiac Unit and as Robert was in London, Jimmy and Sadie stayed overnight and helped out with the playschool run. I got to bed about 9 a.m., alarm set for 12, sat bolt upright allowing the cold to wake me to collect our daughter before 1 p.m. Then on Friday and Saturday nights, we entertained friends and political colleagues.

Our life together now was totally different than the way it had started off in the manse. We now had our daughter to consider in everything we did, and her protection and security was always paramount. While some politicians locked themselves behind closed doors, Robert felt he had to be out amongst the people to be effective.

Like most people in Northern Ireland, life to us was normal but in truth, there was nothing normal about it. What is normal about always looking over your shoulder, not free to walk through any street in your own country, death threats arriving because "they" want you out of the area or just dead. Like so many families, the cleansing was taking place in the Republic and border areas of Northern Ireland.

We had a choice: flee or be driven out, with the third option that was freely handed out—death. So much evil carnage was swept under the carpet by both countries, Republic of Ireland and now our own government.

We wondered many times whether it was a neighbour or someone higher up the chain that set us up as a target. Because of this, we sought to change routines, but you can only change so much. When possible, the three of us would head off for a picnic and end up in the craziest of places. A layby, a field where a gate was open, just wherever our car was out of sight in case we were being watched. On one quiet Saturday after his advice clinic, we were driving in the countryside.

Robert saw a field gate open and, driving the car into the field, we all got out and were having a picnic. We heard a lot of noise coming towards us but due to the high hedges we could not see what it was.

Suddenly, massive machinery came into the field. We had parked in the middle of a field that was going to be ploughed! We did laugh.

Police were calling at our door with ominous regularity.

"We're here to warn you, there's a threat to your East Belfast Advice centre. We'll double the guard!"

Here we go again. For the next few days we were on alert. Checking under the car every time I went out was a useless idea as I didn't know what I was looking for. If there was a lump on the underside of the car, I certainly wouldn't have known whether it belonged there or not.

Then after a few days we'd fall back into our "normal" mode of getting on with life.

Westminster was really getting Robert down. He would say, "Week after week I sit there and work on speeches for the House. Then I sit in the Chamber and wait my turn and try to point out again how many innocent people are being slaughtered in Ulster, trying to get through to those politicians that enough is enough. But in all honesty, they don't or won't see it. They can't grasp the fact that the terrorists aren't interested in anyone's democratic rights or principles.

They are set to bomb, mutilate and kill people until we surrender our beloved province into their hands. They don't understand that we won't surrender. Neither will I stop working against the terrorists because they threaten me. But, Norah, my biggest fear is that if they did anything to you or our daughter or even the dogs, I wouldn't be able to control my rage."

The constant pressure of being elected to the seat of power but finding himself helpless to change anything began to drastically effect Robert.

On his return home, he would be greeted with yet another police or UDR funeral to attend, or another widow to visit and comfort. The toll of lives kept mounting.

Chapter 9

We cannot deny or forget evil

It took some time for me to discover all the perks of Robert's job. For example, I found out there were multiple free warrants for trips to London each year. Only one year did I manage to fit in all the trips I was allocated. It was exciting to visit London and be able to shop for household items or visit Hamley's with our daughter, watching her eyes grow bigger and bigger at the fabulous array of toys. We always went to Harrods at lunchtime, not just for food but to visit the pet department as they fed the array of puppies and kittens. How she loved those times.

Financially, our life was getting slightly better as we had graduated to a Ford Granada which I had taken delivery of when Robert was ill in bed with flu. I had a horrific journey home from the showroom, convinced that it would be scratched before he even saw it. There was some fear in his look when I arrived home and told him I had chosen a car colour that suited us as a family: pink! Whether it was the flu or man flu in hearing it was pink, he struggled out of bed and came to look.

"It's an interesting colour but hardly pink," he said with relief.

We'd had three dark green cars in a row, and I felt we needed a change. This car was a light metallic red with a black vinyl roof. I loved it.

Robert's trips to the southern states of America were now combined with trips to Washington DC to get to know some American politicians. He was always on the lookout to explain what was really happening in this terrorist war (something that was brought to their door in 9-11) and to encourage industrial development in this part of Britain.

On one flight, Robert passed out and ended up in a hospital in Atlanta, so on this trip which we were all going on, I was watching him closely for any signs of illness. The others were sound asleep when Robert squeezed my hand, and I was instantly alert. His face was ashen, and his speech slurred, his pulse slow and weak. I jumped across the prone figures standing on the arm rests and ran to find a stewardess. I asked her to find some brandy as my husband was ill. She fumbled through the drawers taking ages. I ran with it, assuring her I would pay her later and in reaching Robert he was almost unconscious. I dragged him upright from where he lay slumped across my seat and poured a small amount of brandy into his mouth. It dribbled out of the side of his mouth and his eyes rolled upwards. I felt his pulse and was sure he had gone. But gradually his pulse came back and became stronger.

Some of the brandy must have got into his system and turned the crisis around. The instant stimulation of the brandy revived him, soaking into his mouth membranes. I hauled his legs on to the seat to get him horizontal and lifted Claire's sleeping form over the top to lie beside him so that he could stretch out over the three seats. His colour gradually returned, and his condition improved. By the end of the flight, he was still weak but otherwise fine, although I was in a state of shock for quite a while. I didn't like to tell him how close to dying he had come. The problem was obviously the altitude and now that I knew brandy helped, I would keep some on hand.

Doctors couldn't find an obvious cause, and it was some years before diagnosis. When he needed to fly long haul on future occasions, he bought a miniature brandy, diluted it with water, and sipped at it to keep his heart rate stable.

Florence and Webb Bruce had planned a lovely surprise for us while Robert flew to Washington. They drove us from Vicksburg via Biloxi, Mississippi where their son Buddy managed a top-class Hotel. We overnighted there, then drove on through the panhandle where they had booked us into a hotel in Orlando, Florida for two days so that we could visit Disney World. An incredible treat, the experience of a lifetime, although terribly hot with temperatures in the nineties. My niece and I queued up for various rides and then decided to go to the Haunted House. While we were queuing, a thunderstorm broke, and we were soaked to the skin. We decided our light cotton dresses would dry quickly as soon as the sun came out, but we were into the house before we were completely dried out, making the deliberately cold air conditioning seem even colder and the ride scarier because of it.

We had a fabulous time with our lovely, generous friends. The journey back to Mississippi seemed endless, but we stopped frequently for coffee or meals and to stretch our legs. Robert was back from Washington when we returned. My niece sang movingly on the Sunday in Vicksburg church, and I had my first introduction to some of Evie Tornquist's wonderful gospel songs. The next two weeks in Monroe and Marion, Louisiana were electric. Robert commented that after our soloist finished singing, there was little need for him to preach, such was the presence of God.

Robert's sermons tended to be long, but he held his audience spellbound. He illustrated his sermons with appropriate stories from F. W. Boreham's books, or Francis Gray's Friendship books, or drawn from his own childhood experiences, and one could have heard a pin drop. At the close, Robert would make an appeal for people to come to the communion rail and rededicate their lives to Jesus Christ. He would come down from the pulpit himself and kneel in rededication. The Holy Spirit touched many people at that time.

Our daughter was coping well with being up late every night at church, but she liked to mimic Robert. As he waved his arms about in the pulpit, she would copy him in the pew, and I would try to restrain her, which would only make her more determined. She also liked to repeat the last two words of his sentences, along with the appropriate arm gestures. It proved very exhausting for me.

The flight home was uneventful. Robert avoided eating anything and kept his feet elevated the whole trip. I had a miniature brandy in my pocket in case he might need it.

If Robert was in London and I was off from work, I would man the centres. Listening to people's problems for three or four hours was totally draining. One advice centre was in a chip shop, and it was difficult to concentrate if someone was ordering chips or the fact that other people could hear our conversation. A British Legion Hall was where another centre was held. It was here where there had been an attempt to assassinate him. A girl of an unknown age had been asking if Robert would be in attendance, and the canny caretaker had been suspicious of her and phoned the police. They gave chase to two armed men who arrived but didn't manage to catch them. The police foiled that!

One Saturday I was holding a session in a particularly cramped room and had positioned my daughter in a corner with her colouring book and pens as I warned her to behave, when an unwashed, homeless man walked in. She reacted immediately to the unsavoury odour surrounding him, and I had quite a job silencing her protests which would have offended him. With several stern looks and shushes, she wrapped her arms around her face and declared "Aw, Mummy!" with a look of horror on her half-hidden face.

Robert's comment about this particular client was that he usually came in complaining about the mice in his house but that he then had the mice in complaining about him. I laughed at this but knew that underneath it all Robert cared deeply about people.

I had many experiences of Robert's compassion for homeless people and social outcasts. We would be happily walking along a street together when he would disappear into a café and order a meal for a needy person we had just passed.

Night duty had been taking its toll on me and as soon as we saw daylight financially, I quit. It was such a relief to come out of that zombie-like existence. This allowed me to look for a part-time job.

Out of the blue, a post came up in a clinic about a mile from our house and I applied. I was given a week's refresher course and started on the ward two days later.

Back home, I was having a quiet day, having left Robert at the airport for the early morning shuttle flight to London. I collected Claire from school then went into the lounge to light the fire and flicked on the TV.

All I heard was, *"The Rev. Robert Bradford collapsed today on a flight to London and was taken to the cardiac unit of a London hospital."*

The match burnt my fingers as my mouth fell open and I went into a daze. I sat for a few minutes to collect my thoughts and, after the shock wore off, I ran to the phone. I went through a whole string of emotions but mostly anger, wondering why none of his colleagues had contacted me. I hadn't realised the ringer on my phone was faulty and that they had been trying to contact me all day. Frightened and furious, I picked up the phone to make a call, and my sister-in-law spoke. She was coming straight over to me. I phoned Ulster Television and they were able to tell me which hospital Robert was in. Someone eventually answered the phone in Coronary Care, but I could not make sense of what I was being told. The nurse sensibly took the phone to Robert. Tears of relief rolled down my cheeks when I heard his voice.

Despite his protests, I told him I was coming over. The family rallied round and before long my daughter was packed off to Donaghadee, and I managed to catch the next flight to London. Trying to smile as I entered the ward, I saw that he was wired to a heart monitor, and my heart sank as I looked at his ECG tracing. It didn't look good. He seemed in good form, but his hair was annoying him. I managed to persuade the charge nurse to allow me to wash it, and that seemed to settle him. I had difficulty finding a nearby hotel but eventually the taxi left me at a Bed and Breakfast. I hadn't thought to phone through the number of my accommodation, thinking he was over the worst.

The next morning, I arrived to be told he'd had another crisis during the night when his pulse had dropped drastically, and they hadn't been able to contact me. The doctor in charge diagnosed that Robert was in a state of collapse from exhaustion.

I knew that he hadn't been sleeping well for years while away from home, and this doctor urged him to either take a sleeping tablet or a glass of sherry at bedtime. I was allowed to take him home as long as he agreed to rest for some time. The doctor concluded that Robert's ECG was probably normal for him. The flight home was an anxious time for us but apart from feeling weak, Robert was fine. He acknowledged that he rarely slept when away from home which could mean up to four nights a week. We discussed the pros and cons of sleeping tablets or alcohol and decided alcohol was probably the best option since it was hopefully less addictive.

The doctor suggested that a short break away would do Robert good, so he went to Majorca on his own for a week. When he was home, we all booked into a hotel in Killarney for a few days as our American friends, Florence and Webb, were soon arriving. The weather was glorious. The blue sky and sea made for some lovely photos and a relaxing time. Unfortunately, as we had expected, an election was called, and he was back in the throes of it as soon as he returned to Belfast.

Before his collapse, Robert worked every day until all the work was done to his satisfaction, regardless of the hour. After his most recent hospital stay, if he felt ill or exhausted, he took time to rest, realising that he was only capable of getting through so much in one day.

He took time to play with our daughter when he came home in the evening, played football with her, or pushed her on the swing listening to her happy chatter.

He also took this election at a slower pace, not because he cared any less but because he knew he had pushed himself too hard for too long. He won with an increased percentage of the vote. A celebration dinner for the team had become a tradition, and this one took place on May 19, 1979. We had a conservative government with Margaret Thatcher as prime minister. Our only cause for sadness was that the Rt. Hon. Airey Neave, who had been cruelly assassinated, would not be Secretary of State for Northern Ireland. This man of outstanding ability was a tremendous loss to all of us. Having been a prisoner of war he understood what we were dealing with was at a personal level.

Moral legislation, such as trying to make abortion easier, was taking up more and more of Robert's time. Life was sacred for him, and he fought every inch of the way to see God's laws honoured. Pornography was another battlefield. At one stage, he threatened to prosecute a library who held a book showing graphic child molestation images.

Late in August, I had blocked off three days in Robert's diary so that we could have a short break before winter. It was impossible to have a break in Northern Ireland as he only had to walk down a road for people to stop him for a chat. It was a thrill for people to talk to their MP, and Robert didn't like to seem rude. We decided to go to Galway in the Republic of Ireland.

We got as far as Enniskillen when Robert decided he needed to go back to Belfast for a day. The friends we were staying with were going to Mullaghmore to water ski, so we joined them. It was a beautiful, bright summer's day, hardly a wisp of cloud in the sky as we drove into the tiny village. But what was all the commotion with the ambulances and the Garda? The people we had planned to stay with had gone out in their boat as we were late arriving, and had been nearby as Lord Louis Mountbatten[5] and his family were assassinated by terrorists who had blown up his boat. It was August 27, 1979. They set off the bomb knowing that a party of seven was aboard: Mountbatten; his daughter Patricia; her husband, Lord John Brabourne; their 14-year-old twins, Timothy and Nicholas; and Lord Brabourne's mother, the dowager Lady Doreen Brabourne. Paul Maxwell, 15, and a friend of the family who worked on the boat, was also on board. Mountbatten, Nicholas Brabourne, and Maxwell were killed immediately. Lady Brabourne died the next day, and the others survived serious injuries.

The same day in Warrenpoint, 18 soldiers were massacred. What carnage!

The awful state of shock our friends were in emphasised the unbelievable nightmare that had shaken that beautiful day, turning it into complete blackness. Police advised us that Galway was obviously not safe for us just then, so we returned home and flew to London where Robert could do business and still see us.

---

5 Lord Louis Mountbatten, Earl of Burma, great-grandson of Queen Victoria, second cousin of Queen Elizabeth II and great-uncle of Prince Charles. The World War II hero and last viceroy of India was aboard his -29foot Shadow V fishing boat with six others near his summer home in northwest Ireland the morning of the attack.

Due to the murder of Mountbatten in the Republic and soldiers on the same day in Northern Ireland, hatred was rising in England against anyone with an Irish accent. We spoke with careful English accents for those few days as we walked the streets sightseeing. We knew we dare not let it be known that we were from Northern Ireland for fear of being attacked as terrorists.

Men, women and children were being murdered for some senseless, long-forgotten cause.

Robert worked tirelessly at achieving Unionist unity. He managed to stay in contact with the several brands of Unionism and constantly tried to draw the parties closer together. The logical next step was to put his name forward for leadership of the Official Unionist Party. In an interview with the Belfast Telegraph, he stated his reasons:

"I am not an integrationist although I concede that this course might be seen as a logical extension of Unionism. Because it is clear that we cannot really entrust our future in terms of security to either of the major parties at Westminster, I could not lead the party into an integrationist situation."

About Unionist unity, he stated:

"I think it is counterproductive either to be seen to be either reacting to or provoking misunderstandings or, misconceptions within the Unionist family. I would like to see an improved relationship within Unionism in Northern Ireland and an end to the sterile dogfights and perpetual conflicts. I believe we should have a relationship with those parties who want to maintain the Union with Britain."

Together we discussed the implications for Robert in terms of time and commitment and knew it would involve travelling around the country and speaking at the various branches, but we felt that by doing so he could draw them closer together. He knew too that many people in the party felt he would be the right leader, and he was willing to put his name forward. When the day came for leadership voting,

Robert did not receive enough votes, and I was hugely relieved. I knew the extra pressure would have been unbearable for both of us.

We had applied to adopt another child and although it came as no surprise to be refused, it was still hard to cope with, yet it was Robert who took it hardest. It was a difficult time for both of us, but I watched him withdraw into himself as life weighed him down yet further.

As the battle raged on between Robert and the terrorists, he continued in his efforts to make people aware of their fund-raising activities. His attitude was if you can cut off the food (money) you'll kill the beast.

We took every precaution possible but were fully aware that some mornings, we would open the front door or the garage door and be blown up by a bomb hung there by a meat hook. (That was their latest devilish device.) The terrorists didn't care who they killed; they were determined to silence all dissenting voices.

By summer, we decided to chance another holiday in Corfu and as we wandered around gazing in shop windows, Robert would walk in front while we trailed along behind him. Suddenly from nowhere, a solitary, tall, well-dressed Greek man came by waving his arms and yelling in Greek. As he passed us, he deliberately hit our daughter with a whack on the ear.

"What do you think you are doing?" I shouted after him as I gathered the frightened child into my arms. Robert turned around, and I told him the man had hit her for no reason. Robert took off catching up with the man, but the man pinned Robert in a bear hug totally immobilising him. Struggle as he might, he couldn't free himself. The deranged man then sunk his teeth into Robert's neck at his jugular vein and bit hard. I put our child in a doorway and ran down the street, trying to pull Robert free but to no avail. I was frantic, and my next decision was to scrape my rings hard down the man's cheek.

In doing so, he stopped biting Robert yet still holding on to him, lashed out sideways and kicked me hard. Shopkeepers poured into the street and dragged the man off. He ran away leaving us all terribly shaken and not really understanding what had happened. The locals explained that the man had been shouting about his team losing a football match. They confirmed that although the man was well dressed, they regarded him as totally mad. They took us to a pharmacy to have Robert's neck dressed, and I thought of what might have happened if the deranged man had indeed managed to pierce Robert's jugular vein. The shopkeepers urged us to report the incident to the Tourist Board, but the last thing we wanted was any kind of publicity.

I stored the incident away, wondering why such an evil force had been unleashed on Robert. About a month later at home, I had a strange dream which I relayed to him.

"I was standing in a local town square and for no apparent reason I was attacked by a man and you came running to help me. The man pulled out a knife and stabbed you. I woke up terrified, seeing myself cradling your head and not knowing if you were alive or dead."

As winter's cold enveloped us, the threats were still rolling in week by week as Robert worked at compiling more and more information, delivered sometimes from the strangest sources, on terrorist activities.

But he was fighting a lonely battle, and few other elected MPs were prepared to stand out so strongly, as they were all too aware of the consequences of such action. But the threats that were coming to Robert made him more determined. He appeared on television every week, keeping the public aware of the progress he was making, or the lack of it.

David a full-time police constable was assigned to Robert as the year ended. He fitted in with us very well and we felt it a special blessing that he was a committed Christian who shared our faith.

It was difficult to adjust to having someone constantly with us, but David made his presence as unobtrusive as possible.

Robert's plans for a full-time office had begun to take shape and a couple of rooms above a shop on the Cregagh Road were rented.

I started to make curtains and we got new desks, chairs and filing cabinets. By Christmas, everything was in place, and it was arranged to transfer our phone number in January to the office phone. The new office was advertised by leaflets through our constituents' doors.

Robert's secretary seemed to enjoy the office routine and the company of the two extra ladies taken on part-time.

Robert had worked out a system for constituents' problems whereby if he did not get a satisfactory answer in a short time, the issues were brought to his attention again. He was on good terms with the Housing Officers for the Housing Executive, and his success rate for solving constituents' problems was high.

As a family, we loved Chinese food and regularly visited their various restaurants. Over the years we got to know quite a few of Belfast's Chinese community.

The Chinese folk had frequently mentioned taking us to Hong Kong for a holiday, but Robert had always refused to go on the grounds that it might be looked on as a bribe. He consulted a few friends in Westminster and decided it was only a gift for work done. Robert often helped with legal jargon and wrote letters for them and assisted them in any way possible, so he finally accepted the offer. We also thought maybe we could get business investments into Northern Ireland.

We went for eight days, and I had my miniature brandy in my pocket for the flight.

Hong Kong was all bright lights and glamour. It was a fascinating place where everything seemed to happen at high speed. The only leisurely times were meals, and these could last for hours. They were really interesting with six to ten courses, and even though we only nibbled with chopsticks, we often found it hard to finish. Our hosts made sure we saw as much as possible of the city during our short stay. We even managed to get to the border of China. The whole visit was a memorable one, and we made some interesting business contacts.

For some time, Robert had been looking for a flat close to Parliament and two came up for sale. He phoned home as usual one evening to discuss and described them in detail. They both sounded lovely but I advised the third floor one as opposed to the first floor as I felt people would easily notice his weekend absences on the first floor and that it would also be less likely that a sniper could attack on the third floor.

So, we bought the third floor flat and were very excited at the prospect of owning and decorating it. We had booked a week in Devon in August and planned to spend the following week decorating it. We had only been there for a few days when news of the death of Robert's sister Gwen reached us. He travelled home for her funeral and then came back to Devon. He was quite tense and unable to enjoy the rest of the holiday. Back in London, we began sorting furniture and furnishings for the bare flat. Definitely my forte! We took in some cinema visits and outings to parks and gardens.

By now Robert was familiar with the history of the Palace of Westminster where the two houses of parliament sit. The House of Commons was made up of elected representatives, and the House of Lords comprised of peers of the realm, "Lords Temporal," and bishops of the Church of England, "Lords Spiritual." It gave him great pleasure to conduct guided tours to school groups from home.

He paraded them through the vast complex making history come alive with a fund of interesting stories about characters from the past who had worked there. Constituents or friends who called would be admitted through St. Stephen's entrance, then make their way to the Strangers' Lobby to send a green card into the House of Commons to let Robert know they had arrived.

The pomp and ceremony with which everything was carried out really appealed to Robert. The stately procession from the Speakers Chambers to the House of Commons for prayers at 2.30 p.m. was carried out with extreme dignity. At times, when standing in the crowd, he was tempted to spoil the solemnity of the procession by shouting "walkies" as the popular dog training show tag, but his sense of regard for the Speaker and reverence for the stately traditions always held him back.

Our daughter had made a special friend of one particularly tall policeman who was usually stationed in the lobby outside the Members family room. I often watched her scamper towards him through the thickest crowd of people he was attending to. He would see her coming and stoop down at the last minute and scoop her up in his arms to her giggles, never missing a beat of his rhetoric.

The area that the public has access to is only a small part of the vast complex. It also housed offices, restaurants, numerous bars, and a hairdresser, a gymnasium and a travel agency. It was known for MPs who had been there for several years to get lost in it. My favourite place was a balcony that overlooked the Thames. It was a wonderful experience sitting out under the green striped awnings of the House of Commons' tent, eating luscious strawberries, watching the slow river traffic and listening to the chimes of Big Ben.

The Christian prayer group usually met on Wednesdays at 2.30 p.m.

These were times that Robert really enjoyed. With a nucleus of ten to twelve members attending, it remained a very intimate group of believing people who prayed and read the Scriptures together.

The debates in the House were rather more tedious, especially Northern Ireland business. This was the sign for most people to vacate the chamber. In all the years he was there, this never ceased to amaze Robert. We had a terrorist war going on, but other MPs weren't even prepared to stay and listen to the debate.

The ancient method of voting through the "Aye" and "No" lobbies is still regarded as fool proof throughout the world. When a divisional vote is called, members file towards the lobby of their choice: "Ayes" to the speaker's right and "Nos" to the speaker's left. Names are ticked off as they pass a desk, then two tellers, one from the Government and one from the Opposition, count heads. In the early days of 1974 when the Loyalist eleven was first elected, they had immense power because of their combined numbers, especially over a "hung" parliament. They could sway a vote either way. The major parties spent long hours wooing them, but they stuck firmly together and used their power to their best advantage. Northern Ireland business was usually debated into the small hours in those days, and Robert grew very tired of those late-night sittings. He decided he would like a better attendance of MPs so in the early hours he and some others called for a vote and then took great delight in watching the various members who had to drag themselves out of bed to vote at that unearthly hour of the morning.

Even to this day, no one in Westminster seems to appreciate just how evil and sinister an enemy we were up against, much less know how to deal with them. The terrorists were at that time murdering at least one member of the security forces or a civilian each day, which they would describe as a legitimate target as if that made it alright!

It seemed each day that there was a funeral to be attended. Robert found it hard to cope with the pressure of going to yet another bereaved home and being asked what the government was doing to help while he knew that the government wasn't going to defend a country that gave their sons to them in the wars to defend them.

How do you comfort a family that has just lost a loved one, a father that went out to feed his chickens on a farm in the border area, to be crept up on and shot in the back of the head? How do you chat with a young girlfriend who had her life with her boy all ahead of them, to see her heart broken and makeup running down her face, her boyfriend beaten to death, stripped naked and left on a side of a small country road, with a boobytrap under his body to injure those who would rescue it from a hedgerow. Each day the news was the same.

Like many people in Northern Ireland, the pressure was now telling on me too. I would walk down a corridor at work and totally forget what I had gone for until finally I was asked to pull myself together. My GP ordered a month off work and prescribed some mild tranquillisers. I felt guilty sitting at home, especially as I thought that in a month's time our situation would be unimproved. Like those on the frontline in security and hospitals, I would simply have to gather the threads of my life together and carry on.

Chapter 10

When Time is Taken

Another night has passed and the morning of November 14, 1981 broke. Robert had slept well but on waking, the reality of our lives was vivid again. He was concerned how everything was affecting both of us, and he chatted over how our life had been and suggested that I had wasted ten years of my life being married to him instead of marrying someone else and having an easier life. I assured him I had wanted to marry him. He dropped his weary head and nodded - okay.

I reminded Robert that he had yet another funeral that day, Sam Bell's father. Sam and Robert had been mates for years having a joint 21st Birthday celebration.

He decided to wear a light suit, saying his overcoat would cover it. In those days, black was the common colour at funerals, and he didn't want to walk around all day in black. I suggested he wear his black tie, but he proceeded to take his favourite, maroon-spotted tie out of the drawer, the one our daughter had given him. He carefully folded his black tie into his pocket, saying he would put it on after the advice centre.

I fed and dressed our daughter and readied her for Girls Brigade.

Robert didn't eat breakfast.

It was a while before the bodyguard David arrived to escort Robert. Robert puttered around the house with a heavy heart. I knew the concerns he had was outweighing who could he trust with what he knew. He was always asking deep questions that others were afraid to, searching for hidden evils. Behind the scenes he was uncovering businesses and USA bodies that were laundering money to the Irish Republican terrorists and their Sinn Fein movement. Yet another thing that was coming to his attention, which was all so new at that time - sexual abuse with children. It disturbed him when rumours of this nature came to light in Kincora Boys' Home. He felt there were sinister forces at work that were hidden from the public view in many arenas. He became convinced that the people behind Kincora were not just a group of paedophiles. He felt there was, like an iceberg, more hidden than was in the light.

Even when the bodyguard David arrived, they didn't leave immediately.

As I waited on them to leave, I took the dogs out to our front garden.

As I stood there, I noticed our "silly tree" had nearly lost all its leaves.

I walked over to it and had an irresistible urge to tie on those last three remaining leaves. It was then that I was drawn back to a story I loved from my childhood. The story told of a child who was very ill. She had decided that when the last leaves left the tree outside her bedroom window, she would depart for Heaven. In the story, her small best friend climbed her tree and, with his shoelace, tied on the last few leaves. She took courage that the leaves didn't fall, and she got well again. Just a short hour or so later I understood why God went to all the trouble to prepare me and show me that scenario.

Robert shouted, "Bye, love" as he left the house via the door to the garage, and I hastened to call the dogs near me to keep them safe from the departing car. Robert waved as the car departed. I knew he was later than he wanted, with little hope of getting to the funeral which would add extra stress, feeling he was letting his friend Sam down.

He'd held advice centres four Saturdays a month in various locations over South Belfast since he was elected. This centre wasn't far from our home, and I mistakenly thought it was one of the safer ones that he went to. Most of the other advice centres were bordering the edge of Catholic Protestant areas so anyone could access him without fear. A large, green, grass area in the front of this centre made for a pleasant outlook. It was situated in the heart of a government housing estate that was predominantly Protestant, and it was open to whoever arrived to see him.

Just a few days before the shooting, a stranger was spotted within the building reading the notice board and seemed to be taking note of the building layout, while the day before at 2.15 p.m. the Community Centre phone rung and a man asked if Robert would be there the next day, of which it was confirmed he would be.

That morning in Finaghy Community Centre, there was a bit of a racket going on as children from 8-16 years of age were holding a birthday party. With the noise of a children's disco, anywhere else in the world this would be a normal day but not in Northern Ireland.

Ken Campbell, the caretaker, had been working at the community centre for some years. He arrived around 9 a.m. to open the Centre and make it ready for the day ahead. At the same time when Ken was opening up the centre the IRA stole a car for the murder from a family in the Catholic Andersonstown holding them hostage.

Pensioners and some young mums with their children had started to gather around at 11 a.m. to meet with Robert for advice on housing and payments, etc. The people had lined up from outside the double doors, the whole way into the front of the office door, where Robert would sit approximately 15 feet from the main entrance. A normal Saturday clinic where the locals from the areas who knew each other chatted together as they stood waiting to be called.

At 11:15 a.m. smiles came on their faces as they saw the blue Ford Granada pulling into the area with Robert driving and David sitting in the passenger seat.

Robert, as he always did, got out of the car and greeted everyone with a smile. Followed by his bodyguard they entered the building, Robert making ready the little office, where he would sit behind the desk. Two chairs were made available opposite to him for those who were there for advice. Once a consultation was over, Robert would open the door, bidding safe journeys to those he had just spoken to. Around 11.30 a.m. two elderly pensioners entered the office, and Robert bid them a good day.

Normally the bodyguard would stand between the office door and the main entrance door but due to the disco noise, he went outside to have a chat with the caretaker, Ken.

During the past number of weeks, the estate in which the advice centre was operating was being painted to improve its looks. Painters and workmen were coming and going and no one thought anything of this. So, when two men dressed as painters arrived carrying a plank, no one batted an eye. Dressed in boiler suits splattered with paint, they calmly walked up to the entrance of the centre.

Pulling guns from behind the plank, they made David and Ken Campbell lie face down and immediately shot Ken in the back of the head and his chest. I can't imagine the horror those people felt there that day. Ken was murdered in cold blood, and David, who was lying down on the ground beside Ken, wondered if his next breath would be his last.

A third gunman appeared with a Thompson sub-machine gun to keep a watch over the entrance. People inside the building were discerning if this noise was shots or balloons bursting from the disco.

It wasn't long until the people waiting inside saw the first two gunmen running in pass them, one taking position between the entrance to the disco doors three feet from Robert's office. The other man ran to the entrance of the office and opened the door where two pensioners were sitting chatting with Robert. Using the pensioners as a human shield, the gunman shot Robert three times, killing him instantly.

The women and children started to scream in fear for their lives.

Immediately the terrorist ran back and swapped positions with the second terrorist, where in turn, he now pushed the pensioners out of the way, firing another number of shots into Robert.

A ten-year-old boy who saw the shooting ran under a table to hide.

I understand a very brave fifteen-year-old boy threw a chair at the terrorist, shouting to the children to hide. One little girl went berserk and ran off. She was found an hour later, trembling with fear.

The two terrorists who shot Robert raced to a waiting car while the terrorist with the sub-machine gun sprayed the main entrance doors, not caring for anyone. In his panic to get away, he dropped the pistol grip of the gun onto the ground, leaving it behind him. They made off in a brown Mazda Montrose car driven by a fourth terrorist.

Still in shell-shock of what had just happened, the bodyguard fired three after them as they were escaping, an off-duty police officer emptied his revolver towards the car, with one of the bullets entering the back car seat. The car was later recovered burnt out[6] in Republican Andersonstown.

---

6 Terrorists burnt the vehicles to get rid of DNA.

Chapter 11

My Daddy's been shot!

The ringer on our home phone was still faulty, not ringing when it was meant to ring. Police and friends had been trying to reach me with no success. I picked up the receiver to make a call and Bill McAllister's voice spoke in my ear. Bill had been our circuit steward in the Suffolk church and became a Lisburn councillor. He was a great friend.

"Are you okay?" he asked.

"Yes," I replied "Why?"

"There's been some trouble at the advice centre. Please stay there. I'll be right over."

I phoned the local police station to ask what had happened, furious that no one had contacted me and heard in the background, "Get someone over there now. She's home!"

"Please stay there. We'll be right over!"

I had no intention of sitting still!

I gathered our precious daughter on to my knee at the top of the stairs and told her she was going to have to be very brave because I thought daddy had been hurt. We put on our coats and were just about to leave for the nearest hospital when David and an inspector arrived.

As I raced up the driveway to their car, I yelled, "Which hospital have they taken him to?"

"Come inside a minute," David said, pulling me towards the door.

You're wasting time! I thought.

"I need to get to Robert," I said.

David shook his head and tears welled up in his eyes as he pulled me into the house. My knees began to give way, but I fought to stand.

I murmured, "You mean … gone?"

He nodded, tears streaming down his face.

"We can resuscitate him!" I said and took fresh courage.

He shook his head again, and I allowed him to bring me back inside the room. We sat upstairs on the sofa, and he gently went over what had happened. I wasn't even conscious that our seven-year-old daughter was on my knee until she spoke.

"You mean my daddy's been shot?"

I came down to earth with a bump. I held her tight, realising that the full significance of it hadn't really sunk in for her. To her it was a bit like Cowboys and Indians, when they always got up and ran on, only this time her dad wasn't getting up again.

I suddenly realised how dreadful David looked. I had seen him so often watch other cars if we stopped at traffic lights and on visits to dangerous areas. I had seen him place himself boldly on the side that sniper fire was likely to come from in order to shield Robert. He was no Starsky or Hutch of that day or Marvel character of today, just a "copper" doing the job that had been assigned to him to the best of his ability, willing to lay down his life.

I grasped his shoulders and looked into his tear-filled eyes, "Don't blame yourself."

"But I do!" he said jumping up and pacing the room. "Surely I could have done more."

"If you could, you would have," and I meant it for I knew him well.

"You're no use to your family dead. You know you couldn't have saved him from four of them."

I phoned Sadie and Jimmy to come over urgently as I didn't want to tell them over the phone. I went to the door as they parked their car.

How could I tell them that their only child was gone?

I looked at my cherry tree. There was just one leaf still attached but two tiny precious white blossoms had burst open, where I hadn't even noticed buds earlier. It showed me that the Lord was in charge. He had known way before the evil plans that had been hatched and had been preparing my heart.

As I waited at the door for my in-laws to park their car I prayed, "Thank you, Lord, for today. I don't understand but I know I must thank you in faith and that someday I will understand why. You promise to turn everything around for good to those who love You and walk according to Your promises (Romans 8:28). Somehow, You will turn this to good."

Someone had called at Sadie and Jim's home and told them. They arrived subdued and quiet. I hugged and brought them inside.

Brian Quinn found me standing in the kitchen doorway and asked if he and Chris could take our daughter. She was too young to cope with the trauma and craziness of our home packed with people, most of whom she didn't know. She couldn't even take in all that was taking place, whereas at their home, she could chat and grieve with her best mate and then run and have fun. She could phone me anytime she needed to chat.

Of course, I agreed with relief. It was an ideal solution. I was so grateful. She would be hidden away. She wouldn't be found by any rouge reporter wanting a sensational photo of Robert's grieving child.

The house filled with people very quickly, and my family arrived laden with food to feed the massing crowd. They took over the kitchen, and tea and coffee were poured by the gallon. They were so lovely just doing all they could do, my sister, sisters-in-law, nieces, friends, and brothers helping with arrangements behind the scenes. I wasn't allowed to help. I realised quite quickly that I needed to talk to all the people I could. That was why they'd come. For two days they streamed in.

They needed "a piece of me" for all the best reasons. I would divide myself between the two populated rooms, speaking to everyone in turn. As soon as I came into a room there was an audible sigh of relief.

They could see for themselves if I was okay, then they would be.

Dermot, my brother, appeared and stayed throughout, when a phone call came through from the Queen's office. He took the call.

I was stunned and thrilled that our Queen would send us a personal message.

Dermot had a job where his impartiality was necessary. He stayed by my side, even though to be aligned with a sister who was married to a radical politician might have cost him everything.

Robert's murder caused extreme tension. Republicans were waiting on a backlash from the loyalist paramilitaries and even the ordinary nonviolent loyalist was now seeking action. I felt that it would take very little to make the lid blow off, and only the high regard with which Robert was held by everyone, and the knowledge that he had been striving for so long for peace, stopped a retaliatory backlash.

News of his death had been flashed around the world.

Friends in Australia and America were on the phone within hours, having heard it on their own newscasts. Missionaries in far flung outposts wept for the loss of a friend. Telegrams and people streamed into the house, including Protestants and Catholics from right across the political and social spectrum. Yet that same day, another UDR man was murdered. Terrorists were pushing to try and burst the banks of the river of emotion that was sweeping the province. There were television crews vying for interviews, so we narrowed it down to one person who had been to our home a lot, and I agreed to do an interview. Seated in my own lounge, it was strange to be the one in the limelight where it had always been Robert. I was aware that the country was on a knife edge and felt that anything I could do to prevent all hell breaking loose was at least worth a try.

I appealed for calm, reminded folks that Robert abhorred violence and, to honour him, I requested calm restraint no matter the provocation. I asked that no one else die. I wanted no other home to be in the situation that we were in.

"Please" I pleaded!

Robert and I had discussed his funeral arrangements for we both knew in our hearts that it was only a matter of time. I organised it as he had requested even though I had threatened him at the time that I would do it my way and that he wouldn't be in any position to object.

But at the end, I gave in to my beloved's request. In forty cities, towns and villages throughout Northern Ireland, memorial services were planned for Tuesday lunchtime, to coincide with Robert's funeral in Dundonald Presbyterian Church. These memorial services had a multiple purpose: to remember Robert and to lay wreaths for all the police, UDR and civilians who had been killed in this and in previous wars; to protest at the Government's security policy in our wee country and perhaps, more importantly, to turn to God for release from the unbearable anguish in so many hearts. Tributes to Robert appeared in the press but one summed it all up: *"Greater love hath no man than to lay down his life for his friends"* (John 15:13).

Over 15,000 people attended the Belfast City Centre service at the cenotaph with shops and offices closed for an hour to allow employees to attend. Traffic ground to a halt as crowds spilled over on to the streets with workers from Harland Wolff Shipbuilders and Shorts Plane makers, marching four abreast in their thousands through the Belfast streets, headed by a Union Jack, to pay their tribute.

At least 75,000[7] people met quietly and with great dignity at various war memorials and town squares where they sang hymns, stood silent for two minutes, and joined in earnest prayer for their beloved country.

Flags were lowered to half-mast across the country. I had the feeling that if there had been cranes along the route, they would have bowed as they had for Sir Winston Churchill's funeral, so great was the country's feeling of loss.

---

7 These numbers represented one in ten of the working population of Northern Ireland.

Dermot had slept overnight in our home and stayed by my side throughout. The coffin rested in our spare room and in the middle of the night I went in there. Robert had struggled with claustrophobia, so I unscrewed the heavy lid and slid it sideways. Thick makeup covered his face hiding bullet entry points, but his hair was a real mess. I almost laughed, probably hysteria rising. "You must be horrified," I chuckled and sobbed quietly. I was tempted to tackle it but if I put water to the frizz, what would be the result to the make-up? Reluctantly, I left it alone, eventually revisiting that oh so empty bed.

I showered and dressed in a black and white dress that I'd made for my nursing reunion in September, and I topped it with the mink fur coat that Robert had bought me in Corfu. It had been so strange to try on multiple fur jackets in sweltering heat.

Today, I needed to look my very best for Robert, for My Father God and to honour my family. So, hair and makeup carefully in place, Dermot firmly gripping my hand, we walked to the front gate and waited that crisp, clear winter day. There were cameras flashing and reporters vying for the best shot of the coffin trundling out, and of me, the "widow."

It was so quiet. The car engine was barely audible, and the streets were deserted! Why were we going through Belfast city centre? I had no idea. It was eery still! MCB and Queens University folks were standing quietly on the pavement. I just took it in! In the city centre, there were crowds of people and the same stillness, as those quiet cars floated through, as though on a cloud of prayers.

Gliding out of Belfast centre, Newtownards Road folks stood silent, arriving at Dundonald. The pavements were crammed thick with silent folks spilling out onto the road and up the short hill to the church.

I arrived in the vestry and was made aware of a disturbance earlier which had upset family members. Government representatives arriving were heckled by folks who were so angry that Robert hadn't been kept safe. The church itself was packed to capacity with people crammed into the foyer and stairs. I was led through a side door and took my seat. Robert's folks had wanted to drive their own car and were already seated, my Mum and family coming in beside me.

The coffin was draped in the Northern Ireland flag, the Red Cross of St. Patrick on a white background. On top lay the bunch of flowers that my daughter had picked at her Granny's and Marion's Garden and sent for her dad. The cross-shaped wreath of red carnations and roses from me lay beside it. Many other wreaths were placed on the cars ready to go to the cemetery.

Rev. Roy Magee led a service of praise and thanksgiving to God for his infinite mercy and love. Then Rev. Ian Paisley MP read a passage of Scripture.

The people's love and prayers enveloped me and continued to hold me. Outside the Church as we waited for the coffin, I hadn't thought, "Did I want to walk behind the hearse for a bit?" I didn't know but I decided that "No" was the right choice. I do remember standing on the tarmac gazing up at the clear, crisp, blue sky and feeling the Lord's presence holding me.

As we drove out of the church car park, the roads were still lined with vast numbers of people who had gathered outside the church to listen to the service as it was relayed by a loudspeaker. Along the dual carriageway to Newtownards school, children lined their school fences, as the hearse containing Robert's earthly shell moved slowly to its resting place. The cars quickened as we left Dundonald and when we reached Newtownards, there were more crowds. Policemen controlling the crowds saluted as the hearse passed, some with tears rolling down their cheeks.

At Ballyvester, the car slowed to turn into the cemetery. I noticed a very beautiful fishing boat anchored in the tiny bay, gently rolling in the calm waves.

Strange, I thought, *I've never seen a boat anchored there my whole life.*

Later I discovered it was deliberately done as a mark of respect for Robert.

We drove up the rise into the cemetery.

I was so thankful for such thoughtful friends and family. Someone had realised that Wee Jimmy wanted desperately to carry his son's coffin, so Bill McAllister of similar short stature and other appropriate folks shouldered it with Jimmy from the hearse to the graveside and the service began. People began listening quietly in the chilly air to the words of hope.

Dermot held my right hand, and another large man had my left. He began to collapse so I was having to brace to hold him upright.

A large camera lens was placed onto my right shoulder, and the cameramen pulled downwards with all his strength onto my shoulder.

I didn't turn. I surmised that whoever this was, it was probably part of the television crew flown in to film the church service. Their prime objective, no doubt, was to have me collapse and obtain "wonderful footage" of the grieving widow. By God's grace alone, I stood that day, not a whit moved by the tactics of a very sad, silly person.

What I learnt later was that the local television stations wanted whatever crew was covering this to leave the 12-noon service halfway through so the footage could be aired on lunchtime news. (There was no live feedback then). None of the local crews would do that, knowing how disruptive it would be and how totally disrespectful. A crew was then flown in from the mainland who were willing to do just that. This crew had tried to leave the church service, and the folks in the gallery just closed ranks, and I don't believe they were able to go. I certainly was aware of a slight scuffling noise from that gallery at one point in the service.

The cold, clear, blue sky above restored my equilibrium, and the words of my Father God warmed my heart. People's prayers wrapped around me as the last song was sung over the open grave.

We went to stay with my mother to be alone for a few days. The following Saturday was a horrific day for me as each time I would look at the time, I was reliving every moment of the previous Saturday.

I decided to visit the cemetery, to have some alone time with just Robert and me. Weeping silently, trying to understand, I turned my back on the quiet mound of red clay covered with flowers and, as the sun warmed my face, a thought rose in my heart:
"As Judas Iscariot had a role to play in the crucifixion of Jesus Christ but was insignificant in My final plan, so the terrorists had a part to play in Robert's death, but they are unimportant to My mighty purpose."

I stood very still allowing it to sink in as God spoke to me. The all-powerful King of Heaven had stooped to whisper in my ear.

Some months later, God gave me another verse which sealed his purpose for Robert, and I had it put on his headstone.

BRADFORD

Rev Robert John B.Th. MP
Returned home 14 November 1981 Aged 40 yrs
Precious Husband and Father
"A lovely fragrance, a sacrifice that pleases the very heart of God."
Philippians 4:18 J B Phillips

Robert's work was done but my daughter and I had to move forward.

I needed to get my precious daughter back home and into a sense of normality. She was used to me organising everything as Robert was so often away, so it wasn't too big an adjustment but there was that big hole in her heart that wasn't easily filled.

I needed to pay salaries, sort his office and answer myriads of kind letters and cards.

I threw myself into sorting out Robert's office and answering the hundreds of letters of sympathy. It was easy to be busy during the day, but nights were interminable. Sleeping on the outside of the six-foot bed was not good but the vast empty space left by his absence if I ventured across was worse. Christmas was looming up on my horizon as an insurmountable hurdle. How were we ever going to face it? It was going to need something special to get me through the next hurdle, so the Lord sent an ambassador. Roberta Clements, armed with her latest record "Open My Eyes, Lord," arrived on my doorstep on Christmas Eve. Oh, that spirit-filled music and her friendship gave me the strength to go forward once again, with my hand in His mighty grasp.

My family was wonderful and did all in their power to make our family Christmas together fun. I still laugh when I think of my brother Harold standing with cupped hands in front of him. We were all enjoying playing charades. He would not give up, and finally he admitted, "I've got a lovely bunch of coconuts!" The tears streamed down our faces as we held our sides, the tension of the past weeks washing away!

Some weeks later, when I finally came out of shock, I hit rock bottom.

My friend Noelle had stayed very close the whole time, even walking the mile between our homes over the funeral weekend in stilettos, to help serve the crowds who came to the house when her car was off the road. She did all she could to help me through.

Wee Jimmy and Sadie had a very difficult time adjusting as you can imagine. Dad (wee Jim) went about kicking objects in the garden with his steel-capped shipyard boots.

Robert's Aunt Liz died just a year after Robert, and Wee Jim died two years after Robert from cancer.

Weekends were the worst and for some time, we escaped to Enniskillen to Melanie and Peter Little's home or to Donaghadee for Sunday lunch.

Everyday life was so different. How could I mend my daughter's broken heart? One of Robert's favourite things to do was throw her high in the air. The bit that always got me was that he'd put his arms down before catching her, then she'd scream with delight, and I would remonstrate, "At least keep your arms up!" to no avail. Years later, I showed her a photo of him doing just that and she surprised me, saying, "I don't remember falling out of that tree!" such was the height that he threw her up.

As Christmas passed, I had done many television interviews when a crew came to the house in the snow, asking if I would walk in a local park with the dogs for a "voiceover" piece. I obliged but it was a disaster. I wasn't supposed to look at the camera behind the trees but took the wrong path several times until they were in danger of running out of film. They were very patient.

Talk of the USA trip that Robert was to have gone on began to voice that they wanted me to take his place. How on earth could I do that? I wasn't a politician!

The pressure became stronger and more persistent until I needed to pray and ask the Lord what He thought. I was more than shocked when I sensed that I was to go.

I was invited to Rally's to drum up support for this trip and the necessary finance.

What was expected of me? What would I say? Speeches could be written for me but if I was to speak, then I wanted it to be my words.

The itinerary was settled but I was told that I needed to rest in the middle of the three-week tour. I contacted Florence and Webb and arranged to spend time with them and the church folk we were connected to. They couldn't understand who would want to kill their friend and colleague. That would bring some healing for them and me. Because Northern Ireland has such a short interval between death and funeral, none of them had been able to attend so this would be beneficial for us all.

My daughter was given leave to be off school and would be carefully looked after between family and friends. I had barely eaten in the weeks prior and had lost a lot of weight, so a new wardrobe was much needed for television appearances, interviews with Congress people and Senators, and all that the trip entailed.

We arrived at the airport to find crowds of reporters mobbing the team. Questions of many types were asked, then one inquired, "What does Mrs. Bradford think?"

"Ask her yourself" came the smiling reply, and so began a strange new time for me in the limelight of cameras turned my way, press attention, doors being opened, and a way made.

The TV crew that accompanied us kept the folks at home well informed with what we were achieving. It was a lovely and a dreadful time. Lovely to sense that we were getting the truth through to Americans but dreadful because the attack was very real. Standing in a large, cold hotel lobby trying to sort jewellery from the safety deposit box for the next interview, I felt really weak and wobbly. I told myself that I couldn't collapse here. My jewellery could go AWOL.

Never mind how stupid I'd look. I managed to get back to my room, but it was a tough few days as I fought whatever was coming at me.

There were six locks on each hotel bedroom door, and two on mine were broken. Others in the team had no locks functioning so I didn't feel that vulnerable!

The Press club platform we were seated on was raised so we could see the people seated in the room. I couldn't believe that a priest was at the table of people who had orchestrated a loud demonstration with placards outside our hotel yelling and chanting, "We got Bradford."

Inside the hotel, the ruckus was horrendous from the riotous mob.

Police were having to take turns and come into the lobby for a "breather." I approached one harassed policeman as he drew a breath and bent double, I felt somehow responsible!

"I'm so sorry you're having to deal with this all!"

He grinned at me. "Don't you worry, lady, just let me at 'em!" in his best American drawl.

A priest was now sitting facing me with others at this Press club knowing full well the way they'd behaved, I was horrified. I stared at him unashamed for the longest time! He just stared back most unconcerned.

We did what we felt we had to do in telling the truth to the American people. We were received very warmly and were carefully listened to.

Job done, we headed home. I was not to be involved in politics but to love people and now I had to build a life for our reduced family.

Chapter 12

Living Beyond

It has taken me the full 40 years to come out of the hurt, pain, anguish, betrayal, deception and every other emotion that goes with the territory of having a loved one snatched from the family, never in this world to be held again. My love for the Lord means I know Robert's safe and can't be harmed any further and, in fact, is happier than he's ever been, living, smiling and laughing in the beautiful place called Heaven, totally present with his King.

Very few times in my life have I ever called terrorists by their name (i.e., IRA). The only reason their name has been mentioned here is to help international readers, especially those who thought they were some type of heroes or freedom fighters, when they were really cold-hearted, evil killers who justified their actions with the label they carried. Outside of this I only acknowledge them as terrorists, something this world has seen more and more from 9-11 to further afield. I would never wish terrorism to come to your door, and I would ask on behalf of all the innocent victims of The Troubles: Do not support terrorism no matter what side they are on.

To have lost someone to terrorists and to think murderous thoughts, to want someone dead, or to want them to suffer excruciatingly as I have, is human and justifiable some would say. To do these things in my heart but to choose to repent is to find a better way through. To give myself over to a depraved mindset is to become as them. To stay bitter and steeped in anger, though totally justifiable, would allow me to become the very person that has brought sorrow, grief and horror to us and our land. I want a different heritage for my family.

The generations that come after me will have a freer passage if I walk a Godly way forward and find a way to navigate the pain from the horror of sleepless nights and the flashbacks of killing scenes.

To find the joy of the Lord and His freedom is a deliberate road and one I had to pursue, regardless of the pulls of pain to keep me in the past. Yes, the path to freedom is full of potholes, ditches of anger, and fury that I frequently fall into, but I crawl out, shake myself off (many times just me and the Lord) and move on.

Coming home from the USA in January 1982, I adjusted to being a full-time single Mum.

I was used to locking up the house, paying bills and getting the car serviced. These are many mundane ordinary chores but the whole kit and caboodle on my shoulders was a new experience.

My daughter broke her leg and was off school for some weeks but the flip side of that was we had precious Mum and daughter time.

We moved home a year later and changed school which also gave us a fresh start. Everything in our life had changed. The new area had lots of children, and there was the freedom of local parks and safe cycle areas, plus I had the pleasure of a new garden.

I continually came back to a point of contact with the Lord, repenting of mistakes, and basking in His forgiveness and His peace. And little by little, joy came into my heart, taking one small step, putting one foot in front of the other and trusting all my cares to God. Every step we now took was carefully committed to the Lord, asking for

His advice and guidance. It wasn't always clear but so often God gave peace in decisions and destinations.

As my child was growing and becoming what she was meant to be, I needed to reassess my future. What would be my role now as I'm no longer a wife, no longer a Minister's wife, no longer an MP's wife? Gone were the invitations connected to any of those roles, gone were the dinner parties and a whole set of friends I thought were sincere.

Without much warning, Westminster decided to honour Robert, his work and his standing in Parliament with a plaque (featured on the back cover) in the House of Commons chamber wall, alongside Rt. Hon. Airey Neave MP and others who faithfully served and died.

We travelled as a family to London and, delayed by stringent security, made it just in time for the gathering of our families, friends, and Robert's colleagues, who were seated in the hallowed green benches of The House of Commons. Hosted by the Speaker, the Rt. Hon. John Bercow, we had a speech by Lord Bercow, a prayer by my son-in-law, and then I had to speak. What an interesting and frightening experience it was. The plaque was dedicated with an unveiling ceremony, and we retired to the Speakers chambers for supper and photographs. It would have been over so quickly and would have been such an anti-climax to have just gone to our hotels had it not been for Noelle, who had organised a rooftop bar gathering in the Hilton Hotel for us all.

Refusing to let the terrorists hold me in pain, I looked towards the future and my next step. I decided it was studying. It was frightening and exciting all at the same time. Could I actually do this again and succeed? A new level of joy, fulfilment and terror will sometimes still arise but then I sit back, take stock and remember that the most important person in the Universe loves me and believes in me and has a plan for my life.

I moved into a new job. It was exhilarating and challenging, and I made a whole new set of colleagues and friends.

On the day that I married Robert, my own dad hadn't been there to walk me up the aisle. When the day arrived for my daughter to walk up the aisle, her dad had also been taken. I understood her pain. Yet despite her anguish, I was stunned with how amazingly she faced the day with beauty and grace.

Whether we like it or not, life moves on. People become older, and some say wiser, but who knows? Time does not stop. The young girl Robert and I took hold of as a child now has children of her own. Not only did our daughter lose her father, but the grandchildren lost their grandfather that they never knew.

I wish to close this book by remembering what I wrote at the beginning.

I am just one of many that could tell the story of thousands of people in Northern Ireland and border areas of the Republic of Ireland in mainland UK—terrorists robbed us of a loved one. Nonetheless, I also wish to acknowledge that no matter who you are, pain is pain, and bereavement is the same for all. For the families that have an empty chair and hold anguish in our hearts, to let go of the hurt, anger, hatred, and pain in order forgive seems almost to let the perpetrator off the hook but actually it has freed me to be the person I need to be for my family, the person God means me to be.

Tomorrow, they say, never comes, but what if it did? They may have robbed us of our loved ones but don't let them rob you of your tomorrows with those that love you.

Don't let time be taken.

To invite Norah Bradford or to learn more visit
www.NorahBradford.org

INSPIRED TO WRITE A BOOK?
Contact
Maurice Wylie Media
Your Inspirational Publisher
www.MauriceWylieMedia.com

Specialising in True Life Stories
Based in Northern Ireland and distributing around the world.

For correspondence write to:
Maurice Wylie Media
Blick Studios
51 Malone Road
BELFAST
BT9 6RY